THE BIBLE OF MEDICINAL MUSHROOMS

SAVE THOUSANDS WITH THE COMPLETE BEGINNERS GUIDE ON: PLANTING, GROWING, STORING AND HARVESTING GOURMET MEDICINAL MUSHROOMS TO USE IN YOUR DAILY LIFE

J. P. RAE

© **Copyright 2022 - All rights reserved.**

The content contained within this book may not be reproduced, duplicated or transmitted without direct written permission from the author or the publisher.

Under no circumstances will any blame or legal responsibility be held against the publisher, or author, for any damages, reparation, or monetary loss due to the information contained within this book, either directly or indirectly.

Legal Notice:

This book is copyright protected. It is only for personal use. You cannot amend, distribute, sell, use, quote or paraphrase any part, or the content within this book, without the consent of the author or publisher.

Disclaimer Notice:

Please note the information contained within this document is for educational and entertainment purposes only. All effort has been executed to present accurate, up to date, reliable, complete information. No warranties of any kind are declared or implied. Readers acknowledge that the author is not engaged in rendering legal, financial, medical or professional advice. The content within this book has been derived from various sources. Please consult a licensed professional before attempting any techniques outlined in this book.

By reading this document, the reader agrees that under no circumstances is the author responsible for any losses, direct or indirect, that are incurred as a result of the use of the information contained within this document, including, but not limited to, errors, omissions, or inaccuracies.

CONTENTS

Introduction	7
1. MEDICINAL MUSHROOMS: CAN MUSHROOMS IMPROVE YOUR HEALTH?	13
What Are Mushrooms?	14
Discovery of Medicinal Mushrooms	27
Fun Facts about Mushrooms	31
2. WHAT'S IN THE REISHI MUSHROOM?	33
Benefits of Reishi Mushrooms	34
Reishi: The Mushroom of Immortality	40
How to Grow Reishi Mushrooms	42
3. LION'S MANE: THE BRAIN'S SUPER FOOD!	53
Benefits of Lion's Mane	54
Lion's Mane is a Brain Superfood	60
How to Grow Lion's Mane Mushrooms	62
4. HOW TO LOOK YOUNG WITH CHAGA MUSHROOMS	71
Health Benefits	73
How to Grow Chaga at Home	78
5. SHIITAKE MUSHROOMS: GIVE YOUR HEART WHAT IT DESERVES	89
Benefits of Shiitake	90
How to Grow Shiitake Mushrooms for Just Five Dollars	94

6. FIGHT CANCER CELLS WITH TURKEY TAIL MUSHROOMS — 101

   Immune Boosting Benefits — 102
   Potential Risks — 106
   How to Grow Turkey Tail Mushrooms — 107

7. CORDYCEPS MUSHROOM: YOUR ENERGY BOOSTER — 115

   Benefits of Cordyceps — 117
   How to Grow Cordyceps Mushrooms — 121

8. MAITAKE MUSHROOM: BENEFIT FROM ITS ANTI-TUMOR PROPERTIES — 131

   Health Benefits of Maitake Mushrooms — 132
   How to Grow Maitake Mushrooms — 135

9. OYSTER MUSHROOMS — 147
   Benefits of Oyster Mushrooms — 148
   How to Grow Oyster Mushrooms — 153

10. WOOD EAR MUSHROOM — 173
   Potential Benefits — 174
   How to Rehydrate Wood Ear Mushrooms and Recipes to Try — 178

Conclusion — 185
References — 193
Photo References — 203

"Mushrooms are miniature pharmaceutical factories. Of the thousands of mushroom species in nature, our ancestors and modern scientists have identified several dozen with a unique combination of talents that improve our health."

— PAUL STAMETS

A SPECIAL GIFT TO OUR READERS

With your purchase of this book, we have included a gift to help you prepare for the future. Herbal Medicine 101 will not only let you discover more about herbal remediescommunity but let you get involved in the commu- nity. This is the key to opening the door for starting your journey.

Scan the QR code below and let us know what email is best to deliver it to.

INTRODUCTION

Did you know that mushrooms can improve your cognitive abilities, prevent cancer, and reduce your risk of heart disease? There are even types of mushrooms that can improve circulation, improve gut health, and help us sleep.

Mushrooms and fungi are very polarizing topics. Some people love mushrooms, and others hate them. However, two things cannot be debated: one, medicinal mushrooms are excellent for our health and can be used alongside Western medicine to help treat various illnesses and diseases; two, when consumed regularly, they can help to improve your overall health and prevent the development of health concerns.

We've all experienced pain and illness at some point in our lives. Whether it was yourself or a family member, we all know the experience of feeling sick or that something is wrong and going to the doctor. Sitting in the doctor's office, waiting for our names to be called, can be an unnerving experience. I've experienced the anxiety of not knowing what is wrong with me and having all the worst scenarios repeat in my head. Traditional Western medicine typically treats the symptoms of the problem rather than the underlying issue that is causing the problems in the first place. By not treating the root cause of the symptoms, we know that healing can't happen, and any treatment given will only be temporary. Going to numerous doctors and finding no solutions makes it easy to lose trust in Western medicine. Also, multiple visits and treatments can be very costly.

There are numerous reasons why someone might need to frequent the doctors, including having a weak immune system that makes them more susceptible to the common cold and flu. Others might have developed severe illnesses such as chronic inflammation and cancer. In the case of these severe health concerns, it can be stigmatized that holistic and natural approaches cannot help with their treatment.

Experiencing pain and discomfort or seeing those you love in pain is heartbreaking. Trying to reduce the

Overall, the pain and hurt we feel throughout our lives is a goal that everyone should strive for. After all, being sick is the worst. It feels like we aren't in control, so why wouldn't we take steps to prevent ourselves from becoming ill?

Everyone deserves to live their lives to the fullest. Living with any disease makes it harder to do this. Even the healthiest people can become sick or develop some illnesses. How you deal with this and the changes you make to your lifestyle are what matters. Whether you were healthy your entire life and suddenly developed joint pain, muscles pain, or fatigue—or you are someone who has dealt with a health condition for most of your life—reading this book and learning about the benefits medicinal mushrooms can give you what you need to change your life. The information and skills you will know on this journey will allow you to heal the root cause of any symptoms you are feeling.

Health issues are nothing to be embarrassed about. Everyone experiences them, and they are not a sign of failure. I have had my fair share of health issues. When I entered my 50s, I noticed a decline in my health. I was becoming sicker more often. I knocked it down to aging; however, I was becoming miserable. That is when I started to change my life, added medicinal mushrooms, and adopted a holistic approach to life.

Reading this book will give you many benefits, including discovering the magic PSK—a compound found in many mushrooms that can help fight cancer—and learning how to boost your health through nutrient interplay.

Eating medicinal mushrooms or using them for medicinal properties is only one form of holistic or Eastern medicine. It is a vital part of the practice. Eastern or holistic medicine is often not believed to be popular. Numerous celebrities have adopted holistic lifestyles and have newfound health. Celebrities who practice a holistic lifestyle include: Jennifer Aniston, Kim Cattral, Katy Perry, Shailene Woodley, Oprah Winfrey, Lady Gaga, Richard Gere, and Russel Brand. As more people start to try and find new treatments for their health concerns, they are turning back to nature and healing themselves from the inside out.

My career of choice for over 20 years was as a mushroom cultivator, so it wasn't too hard for me to become introduced to medicinal mushrooms; however, I understand that not everyone has the same knowledge that I do. I've spent years accumulating the information you will learn in this book. I've studied and tried some of the most commonly recommended and had some doubts and failures. There were times when I wasn't eating the right mushrooms for my issues, and I wasn't practicing other healthy habits such as getting enough sleep or exercising along with consuming medicinal mushrooms. These trials and errors allowed me to learn everything I will share with you, so you do not need to go through the same issues I did.

Medicinal mushrooms have been used throughout history, and modern science has allowed us to understand how much nature can help us become healthier. Numerous studies that we will talk about throughout this book look at the effects of medicinal mushrooms and show proof at a chemical level of how these mushrooms can help to improve our health. We will discuss these studies in depth throughout the book as we explore nine different medicinal mushrooms; you can get a wide range of health benefits.

Many of the mushrooms we will talk about in this book can be grown at home and harvested. I will walk you through the process of increasing your mushrooms, harvesting them, consuming them, and preserving them. Foraging mushrooms is also possible, allowing you to get even more benefits from spending time outside. You will learn how to identify these mushrooms and lookalikes to avoid.

At the end of this book, you will know everything you need to know about the nine medicinal mushrooms and how to use them to improve your health. Now it's just up to you to turn the page and start learning how to improve your health.

1

MEDICINAL MUSHROOMS: CAN MUSHROOMS IMPROVE YOUR HEALTH?

*E*ating healthy can become very repetitive and tedious, especially if you are eating the same kinds of vegetables repeatedly. One of the best ways to start bringing variety into your diet while still eating healthy is to consider incorporating more mushrooms into your diet. Mushrooms are one of the most nutritious foods that you can eat. They are packed with nutrients and vitamins that are essential for our health.

Mushrooms are good for eating, but they also come with a variety of medicinal uses that have been utilized for centuries around the world. Eating mushrooms with your dinner is not the only way to introduce and use mushrooms in your life. Understanding the medicinal uses, you can get from mushrooms that you grow or buy from the supermarket can help you

Save thousands of dollars in medical costs and help you become a healthier and happier version of yourself. This chapter will explore what mushrooms are, their health benefits, which mushrooms to avoid, and the discovery of medicinal mushrooms and their uses.

WHAT ARE MUSHROOMS?

Like many other people, you might have described mushrooms as vegetables, but this is false. Mushrooms are classified as fungi. In the modern-day, science follows a five-kingdom classification system: plant, animals, fungi, monera, and Protista. However, this is only a recent development. Mushrooms and other fungi were considered part of the animal classification until 1996, when they were finally recognized as their own kingdom.

It might be surprising that mushrooms were classified as animals rather than plants. Scientific studies of mushrooms have shown that animals and fungi shared a common genetic ancestor about 1.1 billion years ago before they split and became the separate kingdoms that we recognise today. The common ancestor showed that fungi are more related to humans and other animals, rather than being related to plants.

Although often called vegetables, mushrooms do not have any markers of falling under the plant kingdom in the classification system. Plants have roots, leaves, and seeds. They also have a different process of creating food using chlorophyll and photosynthesis. Mushrooms, on the other hand, do not have roots, seeds, or leaves. Instead, they have spores that are blown in the wind that allow them to spread. Mushrooms also do not use photosynthesis but rather gather nutrients from other sources.

There are 50,000 known species of mushrooms on the earth, and we can roughly break them into three different categories for this book. The first category is edible— meaning they are primarily used for food. These mushrooms will have lots of vitamins and nutrients, but it does not mean they will be used medicinally. The second category is medicinal mushrooms. These mushrooms have the primary purpose of being used or eaten for medicinal purposes. The third category is toxic or poisonous mushrooms that are not safe for human conception. We will talk about how to recognize these later in the chapter.

When you think about the word fungus or fungi, you might perceive them negatively. Yes, some fungi are molds, yeast, and mushrooms are dangerous to

Humans, but even these toxic ones can be highly beneficial to the environment.

Why Are Mushrooms Good for the Environment?

The most commonplace for mushrooms to grow is on the forest floor, near the base of trees. This is because mushrooms cannot create their own food and use one of three methods to get food. These three methods include saprophytism, symbiosis, and parasitism.

Saprophytism is when a mushroom starts to grow on something that is decaying. Rotting wood, compost pile, and excrement are the most common examples. When a mushroom is growing using saprophytism, it is essentially gaining nutrients and eating by helping to decompose what is growing on. A mushroom growing this way will digest organic matter, aid in composting the material and release nutrients back into the soil.

The following method mushrooms use to grow is symbiosis. Symbiosis is beneficial for both the mushroom and the living organism. If you see a mushroom growing on the forest floor or another living organism, symbiosis or parasitism is used to survive. The difference between symbiosis and parasitism is the process of mycorrhiza that occurs when a plant's root system becomes connected to a mushroom's vegetative system. A plant

Helps to give the mushroom nutrients that it cannot absorb from the soil, while the mushroom provides the plant with water and minerals in exchange. The most significant benefit of a mushroom using symbiosis to grow is that it will get sugars or carbohydrates from the plant that it would not usually have since it cannot transform sunlight into carbs.

The third method mushrooms use to grow is parasitism, which is similar to symbiosis, except that rather than the process is beneficial for both the mushroom and living organism, it is only suitable for the mushroom. Parasitism involves the mushrooms living off another organism rather than helping it. Depending on the species, mushrooms can kill the host it lives on or keep it alive. Honey mushrooms are a great example of parasitic mushrooms. These mushrooms grow on the ground around trees and onto trees and slowly start to kill them. These mushrooms can also be giant, spanning miles. It can take years for these mushrooms to kill a host, but it kills them eventually.

Although some mushrooms are parasitic in nature, most are good for the environment. Mushrooms, from the stage of being a spore to being full-grown, come with numerous benefits, including:

- The spores' primary decomposers, such as

Oysters and shiitake can be used to create insulation. The insulation used in homes is full of chemicals and fiberglass that are harmful to the environment and our health.
- Bioluminescent mushrooms live through consuming phosphorus and can be used to treat contaminated earth. Land contaminated by landmines and ammunition is full of phosphorus. Allowing these mushrooms to grow here can allow the land to be cleansed and accessible to humans without issues.
- Mushrooms are incredibly versatile for the uses you can get from them. They can be made into plastic-free alternatives or products meant to mimic leather.
- Symbiosis created by mushrooms is excellent for treating illnesses in other plants.
  Micro forestry and mushrooms are a match made in heaven. Mushrooms can live off bacteria that would usually be incredibly dangerous to other plants.
- Mycelium, the part of the mushroom that is underground, helps to filter water by removing harmful pollutants from the water and the earth around it. The mycelium also only stops consuming nutrients when there is none left, so

it removes and filters all contaminants or even invasive systems that it might encounter.
- Mycelium can break down hydrocarbons, which are in oil, meaning that when the mycelium is placed into an environment that has been contaminated with oil, it helps to break it up and clean it. Mycelium can also help clean up disasters such as oil spills. Research has also started to look at how mycelium can help with contamination caused by nuclear waste.

Be Mindful of Toxic Mushrooms!

When you are entering the world of mushrooms and fungi, you need to be mindful of which ones are toxic to humans and which ones are not, especially if you are foraging and not buying mushrooms from a reputable source. Typically, when purchasing Mushrooms at a grocery store, there is no need to worry about accidentally purchasing poisonous mushrooms. They would have been inspected and needed to be approved for sale. Common mushrooms to buy in grocery stores include beech, button or white mushrooms, cremini, enoki, maitake, oyster, portobello, and shiitake.

But if you are foraging for mushrooms, you need to be very careful about the mushrooms you are gathering. You don't want to mistake a poisonous mushroom for a safe one.

By appearance, it can be hard to tell which mushrooms are poisonous or not, with some toxic mushrooms looking suspiciously similar to edible counterparts. Here are some of the most toxic mushrooms found around the world.

☠ Fly Agaric or the Mario Mushroom

This mushroom has the classic red cap and white dots that we see in fairy tales and the Mario games, but it is poisonous to humans. It contains Ibotenic acid and muscimol, which attack the central nervous system and cause coordination loss, agitation, intense nausea, sleepiness, and occasionally hallucinations.

☠ Podostroma Cornu-Damae

This mushroom looks like carrots sprouting from the ground and is found in Korea and Japan. It contains a chemical called trichothecene mycotoxins, which can cause organ failure. Other symptoms include stomach pain, low blood pressure, kidney failure, liver necrosis, hair loss, peeling skin, and death if left untreated.

☠ Destroying Angels

The destroying angels mushroom is the most common toxic mushroom that you can come across. It is an all-white mushroom that is typically very small. You have probably seen one of these mushrooms before. It is found worldwide and causes fatal mycetism (mushroom poisoning) because of the high levels of amatoxins it has. Within hours of being eaten, the mushroom destroys kidney and liver tissues, and a person will experience delirium, violent diarrhea and cramping, vomiting, and convulsions before the liver and kidneys start failing.

☠ Autumn Skullcap

This is another tiny mushroom, growing to only about one and a half inches in width. These mushrooms are yellowish-brown or brown in color and grow on and around decaying coniferous trees. These mushrooms are typically confused with sheathed wood tuft, honey fungus, and velvet foot. This mushroom is found in Australia and the Arctic and will cause liver and kidney failure, resulting in death after seven days if not treated. Immediate symptoms include hypothermia, vomiting, and diarrhea.

☠ Deadly Dapperling

With a name like dapperling, you would think this mushroom would be charming, but this mushroom is very deadly and often mistaken for edible varieties. This mushroom will cause gastro-intestinal death and liver failure when left untreated. This mushroom is found throughout Asia and Europe, and in North American coniferous forests.

☠ Death Cap

The death cap is the deadliest mushroom in the northern hemisphere. This mushroom is ubiquitous, being found in Asia, Europe, and North Africa before being brought to North America and Australia, where it is now an invasive species. The death cap has a green-colored cap and white gills and stems. It is often confused with straw mushrooms. About 50% of people who ingest death cap mushrooms die. Symptoms of eating death caps include dizziness, fatigue, nausea, hypothermic symptoms, headaches, vomiting, diarrhea, intense stomach cramps, dehydration, liver failure, coma, and possible death.

☠ Webcaps

Found in subalpine forests in North America and Europe, webcaps are rusty brown or orange in color. After eating a webcap, individuals will experience flu-like symptoms and, when left untreated, lead to kidney and liver failure or death. Unlike the other mushrooms, symptoms can take two days to three weeks to show up.

☠ Conocybe Filaris

This mushroom grows on lawns in the Pacific Northwest of the United States. It has a brown coloring on its conical cap and gills and is commonly mistaken for magic mushrooms. This mushroom is highly poisonous and can cause extreme liver damage. Symptoms are similar to food poisoning and the stomach flu. You can recover from these symptoms without medical attention, but typically they will surface again and be worse, including kidney and liver failure.

How to Know if a Mushroom Is Poisonous

When foraging mushrooms or growing, you always need to be analyzing your mushrooms to make sure that they are not poisonous. There are numerous tell-tale signs you can look for to determine whether a mushroom is toxic or not. Signs a mushroom might be toxic include:

- Umbrella-shaped cap and white rings on the stem (These mushrooms very likely could be Amanitas, which are poisonous)
- Mushrooms with wrinkled and irregular caps or caps that look like saddles
- Sweet-smelling mushrooms are typically poisonous
- Redcaps and stalks

Beginners to foraging, growing, and buying mushrooms will likely find it harder to identify poisonous mushrooms. If you are foraging, you should have some form of a mushroom guide, whether this is an online one or a book. The most important rule you should remember is that if you are not 100% sure the mushroom is safe, do not eat it.

Health Benefits of Mushrooms

Eating mushrooms is always going to have health benefits. You only need to eat medicinal mushrooms to get health benefits from them. All mushrooms will give you some form of health benefit from eating them. Incorporating the mushrooms you buy from the grocery store into your diet more will allow you to see some health improvement. Mushrooms can give us many health benefits because they are packed with minerals, vitamins, antioxidants, and protein.

The antioxidants mushrooms contain are vitamin C, selenium, and choline. Free radicals are a natural byproduct the body produces as it metabolizes food and performs other essential bodily processes. However, when we have a build-up of these radicals, it can be detrimental to our health, causing oxidative stress, harming our cells, and leading to cancer and heart disease. Antioxidants help fight the adverse effects of free radicals in the body. Cancers that the antioxidants in mushrooms can help prevent include breast, lung, and prostate (Ware, 2019).

Mushrooms are packed with B vitamins, including pantothenic acid, riboflavin, and niacin. These vitamins are essential for promoting good heart health. Niacin is vital for the digestive system and healthy skin, riboflavin is necessary for red blood cell health, and pantothenic acid helps hormone production and keeps the nervous system healthy.

Copper is a mineral vital for producing red blood cells and maintaining healthy nerves and bones. Mushrooms contain copper, and one cup of mushrooms can give you nearly a third of your daily intake.

Fiber is an essential part of everyone's diet, and mushrooms are full of the dietary fiber beta-glucan. Beta-glucan helps to improve heart health and cholesterol levels. It has also been shown to reduce someone's risk of developing Type 2 diabetes and regulating blood sugar.

Mushrooms, like bananas, are high in potassium, which helps promote better muscle, heart, and nerve function.

DISCOVERY OF MEDICINAL MUSHROOMS

Medicinal mushrooms were discovered centuries ago and have been around for millennia. Mushrooms have been a part of the Homo Sapiens diet since we were part of small hunter and gatherer communities. Otzi, the iceman who lived about 5300 years ago, carried mushrooms to live in the Alps of northern Italy. Mushrooms are one of the most significant nutritional sources we can have, and when living in snowy mountains where resources are scarce, they would've been the perfect food. The First Nations people of North America used mushrooms such as puffball mushrooms to treat wounds.

Medicinal mushrooms and their uses have continued to evolve just as humanity has. Modern science has taken what our ancestors have taught us and brought it to the next step to create many medicines. Although the antibiotics that we use today are genetically modified, people thousands of years ago were able to treat infections and wounds from mushrooms because they create antibiotic substances that help kill harmful bacteria and control them. Antibiotics such as penicillin are derived from fungi and mushrooms.

It's important to realize that mushrooms did not evolve to be medicinal because humans used them as such. Instead, humans likely evolved alongside fungi as a means to protect themselves from predators. As humans evolved, "we developed receptors, called pattern recognition receptors, that bind specifically to nonhuman derived carbohydrates, proteins, nucleic acids, and glucans" (Stamets & Zwickey, 2014). When we ingest mushrooms, our body recognizes the chemicals that mushrooms release and use them to trigger our immune systems or other processes within the body. Constant ingesting is preventative as it keeps these levels high, making it harder for us to become sick.

The ways that our bodies interact with mushrooms are astounding. The diversity in which we can react to one type of mushroom shows just how vital mushrooms were to humanity's evolution and survival.

Remember that fungi are more related to animals than plants. Because of the genetic relationship that fungi and animals have, it is likely the cause for us to have so many benefits from eating mushrooms.

Mushrooms Used for Medicinal Purposes

With Traditional Chinese medicine, there are 850 species of medicinal mushrooms recorded.

Throughout history, numerous physicians have used medicinal mushrooms to treat their patients. Hippocrates, who lived around 450 BCE and was responsible for creating the Hippocratic Oath that doctors take today, used the Amadou mushroom to cauterize wounds and as an anti-inflammatory.

Mushrooms and fungi throughout history have been used for a variety of reasons. Here are some examples (Fearon, 2020):

- Diabetes and heart diseases were treated for centuries just by consuming more mushrooms.
- Caterpillar fungus is used to help decrease cholesterol and regulate insulin sensitivities.
- The prevention of cancer, hepatitis, diabetes, and congested arteries was treated with the sun mushroom in Japan and Asia.
- The extracts of Turkey tail, polysaccharide-K, and polysaccharopeptide (PSP) can prevent the growth of cancer cells.

- PSP has also been shown to boost immune systems.
- Multiple species of fungi can be used to make chemotherapy drugs such as paclitaxel. This drug treats various cancers, including breast, bladder, lung, and pancreatic.

Consuming non-medical mushrooms have also been shown to have numerous health benefits, including fighting against cognitive decline and treating mood disorders, depression, and addiction.

Mushrooms and Cognitive Decline

Before mushrooms were found to help battle the fight against cognitive decline, studies were already being conducted on how psychedelic mushrooms can treat depression, anxiety, and addiction. Researchers from Singapore were the first to theorize that mushrooms might be able to fight mild cognitive impairment (MCI)

Initial studies in Singapore showed that older people who consumed more than two portions of mushrooms a week could see a 50% less chance of developing MCI. This study looked at numerous types of mushrooms, including shiitake, golden, white button, oyster, canned, and dried mushrooms, and all were associated with decreased MCI levels (Jefferson, 2019). During these initial studies, scientists acknowledged that other types of mushrooms could have similar effects or even better ones.

Mushrooms are full of substances essential for brain function and the growth of brain cells. These substances include scabronines, erinacines, and dictyophorines. Phosphorylated tau and beta-amyloid are two toxic proteins that can contribute to cognitive decline, dementia, and Alzheimer's development when too much builds up in the brain (Cohut, 2019).

FUN FACTS ABOUT MUSHROOMS

Before we dive into specific medicinal mushrooms for you to try, here are some fun facts about mushrooms:

- Mushrooms can range from pennies to thousands of dollars based on rarity and taste.
- Magic mushrooms might help to boost communication in the brain. It is theorized that the sensation of tripping off magic mushrooms is the brain entering a state of hyperconnectivity as parts of the brain that would usually not communicate with each other start to.
- The physical mushrooms on the ground are not the whole organism. Instead, it is the fruit of a possibly massive organism that is mostly.

underground. The majority of a mushroom lives underground as mycelium. The mushroom we eat allows the bigger organism to spread its spores and grow.
- Mushrooms are the only food other than animals to have the fifth taste: umami. Umami is a meat-like flavor that no fruit, vegetable, or grown foods have. There are species found across the world that taste like fried chicken.
- In Oregon, a honey mushroom was found to be the size of 1,665 football fields and weighing nearly the same as 200 grey whales. This mushroom was declared to be the largest living organism on earth.

Mushrooms are incredibly fascinating and often brushed to the side. Many people would prefer to stick with the known, than branch out and try something new that can be beneficial for their health. You now know what mushrooms are and the many benefits you can get from them. For the rest of the book, each chapter will focus on one of nine medicinal mushrooms that can help you save thousands and boost your health. The first mushroom we will focus on is the Reishi mushroom.

2

WHAT'S IN THE REISHI MUSHROOM?

The reishi mushroom is the first edible medicinal mushroom that we will be discussing in this book. It is very common for people who are not accustomed to eating mushrooms to skip them as they walk through the grocery store. But mushrooms, medicinal or not, can be incredibly beneficial for your health in ways that you might not expect. To start this journey off, we will focus on the reishi mushroom and look at all the benefits you can get from it, why it's deemed the mushroom of immortality, and how you can grow, harvest, use, and store your own reishi mushrooms.

BENEFITS OF REISHI MUSHROOMS

The reishi mushroom, also called lingzhi or Ganoderma lucidum, grows in Asia, specifically in hot and humid locations. The reishi mushroom has been used for centuries in traditional Asian herbal medicines. Reishi mushrooms are eaten fresh and made into powders and extracts for medicinal purposes. The numerous health benefits you can get from these mushrooms are associated with the presence of molecules such as polysaccharides, triterpenoids, and peptidoglycans.

Gives a Boost to the Immune Systems

Amongst the various studies performed on cells, animals, and humans about the benefits of the reishi mushroom, one of the most prominent benefits is the boost the immune system receives. Studies on cells showed that the reishi mushroom affects our white blood cells. White blood cells are critical to our immune system's ability to function and fight off infections and diseases. Another vital part of our immune system is Natural Killer Cells (NK cells) that help fight infections and cancers within the body. Chronic inflammation makes the body's immune system start to exhaust. Reishi mushrooms can help to boost the immune system and alter inflammation pathways.

Cancer patients will often experience decreased NK cells and white blood cells as the body constantly fights the disease. Eating reishi mushrooms or taking reishi mushroom extract can help to increase the activity of NK and white bloodcells.

Those that are already ill are the ones that will see a more significant boost to the immune system, but studies of healthy people have shown that those that are healthy can also see an increase. Some studies showed that completely healthy adults might not see any change in their immune system while taking reishi mushroom extract (Tinsley, 2018). This is why it is really important to realize that mushrooms and fungi are not a cure-all and that not everyone will have the same reaction.

Can Fight Depression and Fatigue

An essential part of preventative health care is taking care of our physical health alongside mental and emotional health. Many people do not realize that our mental health impacts our physical health, and the same goes the other way. Mental health disorders that are not treated or managed correctly can cause physical health issues to arise, while non-treated physical health issues can cause your mental health to start to decline. One of the most common physical symptoms associated with underlying mental health problems is fatigue or issues with sleeping.

The reishi mushroom is truly unique as it can help fight depression and battle fatigue. Chronic inflammation can often signify underlying mental health issues alongside physical health issues.

Studies showed the boost to our immune system given by the reishi mushroom can also impact feelings of fatigue and depression. Neurasthenia is a condition that has been defined by feelings of pains, aches, dizziness, irritability, and headaches, which are many of the same symptoms people with depression and fatigue might feel. A study of how the reishi mushroom inter-acts with the conditions studied 132 people diagnosed with neurasthenia. The patients were given supple-ments made with reishi mushroom, and after eight weeks, fatigue and depressive symptoms were reduced significantly, and the patients reported a better quality of life (Tinsley, 2018).

Another study of 48 breast cancer survivors showed that after taking reishi mushroom powder for four weeks, they saw the same reduction in fatigue and a rise in quality of life (Tinsley, 2018).

Studies were not diagnosed on patients who solely experienced depression with no other health conditions, so it is unclear if they would see the same results. It was noted that anxiety was slightly reduced during the studies. No direct studies have been conducted on how the reishi mushroom might treat anxiety-based disorders.

Reishi Mushroom has Anti-Cancer Properties

Reishi mushrooms and multiple other fungi have anti-cancer properties and have been used to create medications specifically for fighting cancer. When someone is diagnosed with cancer, they are always looking for different treatments, and some of them decide that they are going to eat more mushrooms. Reishi is one of the most popular choices of mushrooms when it comes to fighting cancer. A study of breast cancer survivors showed that nearly 59% of them were consuming reishi mushrooms in some way (Tinsley, 2018).

The reishi mushroom was shown to be effective against various cancers, including prostate and colorectal. Reishi mushrooms affect testosterone, making it effective against prostate cancer. Tumors were also affected by reishi mushrooms. A study on how reishi mushrooms affect tumors in the large intestines showed that the number and size of the tumors decreased after a year of treatment with reishi mushrooms.

The increase of white blood cells that we discussed in the immune system section also helps fight cancer cells. A cancer patient should not use reishi mushrooms as a sole treatment but use them in conjunction with other medical treatments. There haven't been enough studies to show how effective reishi mushrooms are against cancer when they are the only treatment method.

Possible Increase in Antioxidants

Antioxidants are vital molecules for the immune system as they protect the health of our cells. The reishi mushroom's effect on the immune system means there should be an increase in antioxidants as well.

However, preliminary studies did not show an increase in antibiotic enzymes (Tinsley, 2018).

As we discussed in the previous chapter, mushrooms are packed with antioxidants, and eating them regularly will increase your antioxidant levels. So, more studies might still be possible to show that the reishi mushroom impacts our antioxidant levels.

Possible Decrease in Blood Sugar Levels

Limited research has been conducted on this benefit, but preliminary studies on animals and humans showed that the reishi mushroom impacted blood sugar levels. It was found that some molecules within the reishi mushroom might decrease blood sugars. Animal studies did show this effect.

Studies conducted on humans have been very mixed in terms of results. The results were all over the board, with some of the patients seeing the desired decrease and others having a worse effect than those given a placebo.

Possible Improvement in Heart Health

Cholesterol is split into two categories; good and bad. Good cholesterol or high-density lipoprotein (HDL) helps to absorb bad cholesterol and bring it to the liver, where it is flushed from the body. Bad cholesterol is responsible for clogging arteries and increasing the risk of developing heart disease. Triglycerides are one type of fat found in the body and can increase bad cholesterol.

In studies, the reishi mushroom has increased HDL and decreased bad cholesterol. One study showed that after 12 weeks of consuming reishi mushrooms, 26 people saw their HDL levels rise, and triglycerides decreased (Tinsley, 2018).

However, studies have directly counteracted research claiming reishi mushrooms affect heart health. These showed that patients saw no decrease in cholesterol levels and no change in their risk of developing heart disease.

REISHI: THE MUSHROOM OF IMMORTALITY

Reishi is one of the most prevalent medicinal mushrooms used in the growing phytomedicine industry. It has been used to promote general well-being and longevity for many years, which has led to the listing of the substance in various Compendiums and Pharmacopoeias worldwide. Reishi is believed to be the mushroom of immortality in many cultures. Reishi has a distinct appearance, identified by the iconic kidney or fan-shaped cap, with a reddish hue and shiny surface. This fungus is a saprotrophic mushroom that feeds on dead organic matter, which means you will be able to find this species in areas where hardwood stumps and logs like oaks and maples are present. Be on the lookout for any old tree stumps, logs, or dying trees in a forest or woodland in the Eastern regions of the northern hemisphere, such as Japan, China, and Korea.

Reishi possesses a wide range of medicinal functions and pharmacological properties, which ultimately support longevity. This is possible due to the two main groups of metabolites, which are referred to as triterpenoids and polysaccharides, respectively. These metabolites contribute to increased immunomodulation and immunostimulation, but can also be used as a supplementary compound for cancer due to their anti-cancer properties.

Reishi mushrooms could become an essential addition to your diet since they contain antioxidants, essential nutrients, and minerals. It is a healthy source of the primary B complex vitamins, consisting of thiamine, folic acid, niacin, thiamine, and riboflavin. There is also a generous amount of protein found in the mushroom.

Based on average, the amount of protein present in reishi equates to approximately 19.5mg for every 100 grams, which is a considerable amount higher than the common Oyster mushroom. Additionally, the protein consists of various essential amino acids, which places this mushroom on the priority list of any vegan or vegetarian diet as a healthy source of daily protein requirements. It also contains an adequate amount of potassium, a critical mineral for heartbeat regulation, normal cell functioning, and improved nerve signaling. In addition to the presence of vitamin D, another essential nutrient may contribute to the construct of specific white blood cells, known as Selenium. This, in turn, means reishi could assist with regulating the immune system.

HOW TO GROW REISHI MUSHROOMS

Growing reishi mushrooms is incredibly easy, and it is also inexpensive, making it perfect for beginners who are learning to grow their own mushrooms. Reishi mushrooms are quick to colonize and are sturdy against contaminators that might kill them.

Materials needed to grow reishi mushrooms:

- reishi spawn
- large bucket

- boiling water
- substrate made from 50% course and 50% fine hardwood sawdust
- plastic wrap
- optional: 2% calcium carbonate and gypsum

Reishi spawn is needed to add to the substrate, which is required to grow them. There are multiple places online where you can buy reishi spawn. When purchasing reishi spawn, there are three types that you can buy. I will tell you that the steps for growing reishi mushrooms require grain or sawdust spawn. Grain and sawdust reishi spawn are the least expensive and considered the more accessible versions to grow with.

Follow these five easy steps to grow reishi mushrooms:

1. Pasteurize substrate. The substrate is the material in which your mushrooms are going to grow. You can make or buy substrate, but if you do, make sure that it is equal parts coarse and fine hardwood sawdust. Add the 2% calcium carbonate and gypsum if you want a higher yield.

- Drill small holes near the top of the bucket to drain water.
- Put the sawdust and optional materials into a

bucket and mix, but ensure you are not filling it completely.
- Submerge the substrate in boiling water and let sit for two hours.
- Drain and ensure there is no excess water. If there is any excess water, mould might
- grow. Cover and let the substrate sit for eight hours before moving on to the next step.

2. **Spawn the substrate.** After waiting eight hours, check to ensure the substrate has cooled to below 35 degrees Celsius.

- If the substrate is still not cooled, allow it to cool. A substrate that is too warm will kill the mushrooms.
- If the substrate is cooled, mix in reishi spawn to evenly incorporate it.

3. **Wait for mushrooms to grow.** Once you have added the spawn, cover it with plastic wrap. Make sure the holes are not covered. If you think you need to, poke holes into the plastic wrap.

- Store the bucket in a dark and warm area.
- After a few days, you might see a thread-like growth, and about 15-20 days after adding

spawn to the substrate; you will see your mushrooms growing.

4. Fruit your reishi mushrooms. The substrate will be covered in a similar growth to cobwebs when it is colonized.

- Move the bucket into a well-lit area that is cool and airy.
- Keep for another two weeks, and then remove plastic wrap.
- Spray mushrooms two to three times a day.

5. Harvest your reishi mushrooms. It will take several weeks for the mushrooms to reach maturity.

- When the mushrooms appear red, in a fan shape, and have a wet lacquered appearance, they are ready to be harvested.

How to Harvest Reishi Mushrooms

Harvesting reishi mushrooms is very easy. Sadly, unless you live in certain parts of Asia, you will not be able to go out and forage for reishi mushrooms. To harvest your reishi mushroom, you can cut them from the substrate or gently pull them away. Before removing them from the substrate, look at the undersides of the mushrooms. The perfect time to harvest is when the underside is white. When your mushrooms have reached maturity, they will be red and have a lacquered appearance. This means the mushroom is still relatively young and will be full of nutrients. You can still harvest them if they have passed this stage; however, you need to understand that older reishi mushrooms can hold mold, and the flavor and texture will be altered. An older reishi mushroom will be more bitter and the texture tougher.

Use a toothbrush or damp towel to remove any dirt from your reishi mushrooms. Do not submerge the mushroom because it can absorb the water, making it harder to use and leads to molding.

How to Use Reishi Mushrooms

Two forms are the most popular when using reishi mushrooms for medicinal purposes. The first way reishi mushrooms are used medicinally is by making a powder. To create this powder, reishi mushrooms are dried and then crushed. You can use this powder in various ways, including sprinkling it into soups and stews.

The second way reishi mushroom is consumed for medicinal purposes is through making tea. The tea can be made from fresh or dried reishi and stored in the fridge for several days. However, be prepared for an extremely bitter taste.

Cautions

As with any medicinal mushroom, herb, or medication, there are always possible side effects and cautions that need to be taken. Studies revealed that consuming reishi mushrooms medicinally for more than four months made people twice as likely to develop side effects (Tinsley, 2018). Using reishi mushrooms for medicinal purposes should not be done for long periods of time.

Most of the side effects of eating the reishi mushroom are not severe, including an upset stomach or some form of digestive distress. However, there have been causes of people experiencing problems with their kidneys and liver after using reishi powder for an extended period. In a series of studies, there were two cases where people reported having issues with their liver. Both of these individuals had eaten reishi and used it in other forms without problems, but when they were switched to the powder form, they started to experience side effects (Tinsley, 2018). It is possible that the powder extract was more potent than other forms, causing these people to have adverse reactions.

If you are breastfeeding, have low blood pressure, are undergoing surgery, or have a blood disorder, you should avoid using the reishi mushroom. Extreme side effects might include dryness around the mouth, throat, and nasal area, itchiness, rashes, nose bleeds, and bloody stools (Tiny Plantation, 2017). If any side effects occur, stop using reishi mushrooms immediately and seek professional care.

Proper Dosage

When buying reishi powder, the recommended dosage should be on the packet, and it will change based on your health, age, and other possible conditions that you might have. Dried reishi is much more potent than fresh reishi, so powders will have a minimal dosage compared to if you are eating the mushroom fresh.

Depending on the variants we talked about, the typical dried reishi mushroom extract dosage ranges between 1.5-9 grams a day. Fresh reishi mushroom dosages will be ten times higher than their powdered counterparts. If you take a dosage of about five grams of reishi powder, this will equal about 50 grams of fresh reishi.

When growing your reishi, consult a physician about how much you should be using and for how long they would recommend you do.

How to Store Reishi

Reishi mushrooms spoil quickly, so you will want to preserve or use them immediately after harvesting. Drying your reishi mushrooms is one of the best and most accessible options. Cutting the mushrooms into slices will allow the mushroom to dry quicker and properly as the mushroom can be too thick otherwise. There are multiple ways to dry your reishi mushrooms, including laying them in the sun, using a food dehydrator, or oven at the lowest temperature. Store your reishi mushrooms in an air-tight container for up to a year after drying. After you have dried your reishi mushrooms, you can use them in many ways.

How to Cook Reishi Mushrooms

Reishi can be consumed in its original or fresh form; however, it has been reported that its texture is rather tough and similar to rubber, which makes for an unpleasant experience when you try to consume it. The mushroom taste has been explained as having savory flavors with a slight bitterness, which means the powdered form of the mushroom could be used as a balancing agent for any dessert if the sweetness is too potent.

Looking at various alternative consumption methods, this substance will be pretty versatile. Numerous ways

To consume reishi mushrooms include capsules, tincture, powdered, and dried.

Tinctures can be made by adding fresh reishi to alcohol or vinegar, and for reishi, it is recommended to do a double extraction tincture. To make a double extraction tincture, follow these steps:

1. Chop fresh reishi and add to a jar with vinegar or alcohol. If using alcohol, it should be between 25-30%. Keep in alcohol for a month, shaking daily.
2. Strain mushrooms, then set liquid and mushroom aside.
3. Boil water and add mushrooms. Allow the mushrooms to simmer for two hours or until the water has mostly reduced.
4. Allow cooling before straining mushrooms.
5. Combine alcohol and water in a container, and you have your double extraction tincture.

You can create reishi powder by grinding up dried reishi. This powder can then be used to make tea or added to soups, stews, or smoothies for added nutrients. Tea can also be made from powder or dried reishi slices. Reishi mushrooms can also be prepared fresh and have a texture similar to tofu. However, they can become flavorless during the cooking process, so you will want to enhance their flavor with other herbs and spices.

The reishi mushroom is a great starting point for anyone trying to grow their own medicinal mushrooms while also getting some excellent health benefits. Improving your physical health is only the start of your journey. In the next chapter, we will discuss a mushroom that will enhance your brainpower. And that is the lion's mane.

3

LION'S MANE: THE BRAIN'S SUPERFOOD!

Do you experience brain fog? Find that you can't concentrate or focus throughout the day? Don't worry. You are not alone! Everyone at some point in their lives experiences brain fog. The amount can differ day to day and can be influenced by many things, including, mental health, physical health, lack of sleep, diet, and many other things. Doctors can prescribe medication, but they often do not work because they do not work at the underlying cause of your brain fog. Lion's mane prefers to grow in climates with low to moderate temperatures in the lowlands of tropical environments. It produces a white clump of rot with dangling spines on dead hardwood tree trunks. With a taste resembling seafood, this mushroom is an excellent culinary addition. Lion's mane is a mushroom with multiple benefits for mental and physical health, which can help improve your cognitive abilities and mental clarity. This chapter will explore the benefits of lion's mane, how to grow it, harvest it, and consume it.

BENEFITS OF LION'S MANE

The lion's mane mushroom is renowned for its effects on our brain functioning. It also has positive effects on our physical health, which I will go through in this section, but the real focus of the lion's mane mushroom is the massive benefits on your cognitive health. This truly is a mushroom that attacks cognitive and mental decline from all angles.

Can Relieve Symptoms of Anxiety and Depression

Remember that cognitive decline can be caused or worsened by symptoms of anxiety and depression. It can be hard to determine which one causes the other because it can differ from person to person. Someone might be experiencing these symptoms because of cognitive decline resulting from these symptoms. It is different for each person, but that's where the lion's mane comes into play. It can help to relieve these symptoms while also improving cognitive function.

Anxiety and depression are by no means uncommon. It is estimated that about one-third of the population in developed countries experience symptoms of depression and anxiety (Julson, 2018). There are many causes for this, chronic inflammation being one of many. However, it is essential to understand the cause of your symptoms because even though you might have some relief from these symptoms, the lion's mane is not a replacement for professional help if that is what you need.

Depression and anxiety symptoms caused by chronic inflammation will experience the most significant decline. The lion's mane mushroom reduces these symptoms through its anti-inflammatory and immune-boosting properties. Studies on mice showed that lion's mane extract could reduce depression and anxiety symptoms because of its anti-inflammatory properties (Julson, 2018).

The hippocampus is the brain area where emotional responses and memories are processed, and it becomes impaired when experiencing anxiety and depressive symptoms. The anti-inflammatory and immune-boosting properties of the lion's mane have been shown to help regenerate brain cells and improve the functioning of the hippocampus, which can help relieve the symptoms of depression and anxiety and enhance memory formation (Julson, 2018). However, this study has only been done on animals, so it is theorized that the effect on humans will be similar.

One study on menopausal women who reported feelings of anxiety and irritation showed a reduction in these feelings when they ate cookies with lion's mane mushrooms daily (Julson, 2018).

The decrease in these symptoms then helps to improve one's ability to focus, concentrate, and process memories. The brain's ability to process memories is hindered when someone is experiencing mental health issues, so mental clarity and memory formation will be back on the rise when these symptoms are reduced.

Can Protect Against Dementia and Alzheimer's

Ageing and losing your cognitive abilities is the fear of many people. You might be one of these people. If you have a relative with dementia, you know how damaging it is to yourself and those around you. One of the ways you can protect yourself from dementia is to introduce more lion's mane into your diet.

Dementia forms because the brain cannot make as many connections as we grow older. When this ability is severely diminished, the existing connections start to wither and are not renewed with the new connections.

This causes memory loss and confusion associated with dementia or Alzheimer's. Stimulating brain cell growth will help deter these effects, and lion's mane mushrooms have two compounds that do just that. Erinacines and hericenones are compounds in the lion's mane mushrooms that help to promote brain cell growth which fosters the creation of more connections. When the brain makes a new connection, it reinforces what it already knows and introduces further information.

Amyloid-beta plaque buildup is a sign of someone entering the early stages of Alzheimer's. This plaque then causes neuronal damage, which prevents the brain from making connections and causes memory loss and neurological degeneration. Studies on mice showed that lion's mane mushrooms could protect against the damage caused by amyloid-beta plaque (Jul·son, 2018).

Boosting cognitive and mental functioning is the best way to stop the degeneration of their abilities as someone grows older. We sometimes don't notice a decline until it has become severe, which can be hard to recover from. However, lion's mane mushrooms have been shown to boost mental functioning, which can help clear brain fogginess and improve cognitive abilities, allowing the brain to kickstart itself back into

Making connections, which can improve mental function down the line and protect against dementia.

Lion's mane effectiveness, though, is not infinite. People with mild cognitive impairment will see more results than those with severe cognitive impairment. A study on older adults showed that taking a lion's mane supplement positively impacted their cognitive functions. However, these effects stopped when the patients stopped taking the supplements (Julson, 2018). This showed that the effects were dependent on a constant exposure rather than short-term.

Can Speed the Recovery Time of Nervous System Injuries

When we think about injuries typically, we think about physical injuries, but our nervous systems can also become injured. The nervous system contains the brain, nerves, and spinal cords. Our nervous system is responsible for sending and receiving signals for various bodily functions. When there is an injury to our nerves, brain, or spine, it causes the nervous system to become impaired. Brain injuries can be extremely devastating to cognitive functioning. These injuries can take a long time to heal. Lion's mane mushroom was shown in studies to help speed up the recovery of nervous system injuries as it promotes the growth and repair of nerve cells. For rats with this type of injury, studies showed that their recovery was 23-41% faster when given lion's mane extract than those not (Julson, 2018).

By promoting the repair and growth of nerve and brain cells, the lion's mane mushroom can help to reduce brain damage caused by strokes. A study with rats showed a damage reduction of nearly 44%, along with a decrease in inflammation (Julson, 2018).

Physical Health Benefits of Lion's Mane

The lion's mane mushroom comes with various physical health benefits. Like all mushrooms and fungi, the lion's mane is chock full of nutrients and vitamins that will give an array of benefits. This mushroom also has anti-inflammatory and immune-boosting properties to strengthen your immune system and reduce the risk of various diseases, viruses, or illnesses. The physical health benefits of consuming lion's mane mushrooms include:

- reduces the risk of heart disease
- stops the formation of digestive tract ulcers
- and lessens regular symptoms of diabetes
- helps fight cancer.

LION'S MANE IS A BRAIN SUPERFOOD

There are multiple reasons you might be experiencing cognitive decline, no matter your age. Yes, older people have a greater chance of cognitive decline and developing diseases such as Alzheimer's and dementia. Still, various factors can lead to a reduction in cognitive abilities even from a young age. Healthy habits such as eating healthy foods, getting enough sleep, and exercising are some of the best habits that you can practice. Lion's mane is one of the best mushrooms you can start to eat that will help provide nutrients that can boost your cognitive health and keep your nervous system healthy.

Regarded as the ultimate brain booster, this powerful neurotropic doesn't have the side effects of the widely-accepted stimulants most people use daily. The Hericium Erinaceus, or Lion's Mane mushroom, contains two groups of compounds (erinacines and hericenones) which can easily pass through blood vessels and the membrane of the brain. This allows the compounds to promote nerve growth factor synthesis and protect the brain against neurodegeneration. Aside from its everyday use for increased cognitive clarity, this mushroom's medicinal value also dramatically benefits the recovery of peripheral nerve injury and even tissue damage.

The lion's mane's cognitive superfood abilities come from producing the bioprotein NFG (nerve growth factor) and myelin which is the insulation that forms around nerve fibers. Both of these components are essential for our brain's health, and when these are imbalanced, this is when multiple sclerosis, Alzheimer's, and dementia can start to develop. Eating lion's mane helps balance NFG and myelin, protecting the brain and promoting cognitive health.

HOW TO GROW LION' S MANE MUSHROOMS

One of the most significant benefits of growing lion's mane mushrooms is the culinary uses you can get from them and reap the benefits of consuming them regularly. Lion's mane mushrooms are said to taste like seafood after being cooked, and if you live somewhere here you don't have much access to fresh seafood, this can be a great alternative.

Materials needed:

- lion's mane spawn
- substrates such as softwood or hardwood sawdust, straw, or store-bought substrates that are rich in cellulose
- large bucket
- pressure cooker
- small jars or polypropylene bags or plastic

Follow these steps to grow your own lion's mane mushrooms:

1. Sterilize your substrate. Soak in hot water for two hours and drain excess water. Allow to sit

for a half-hour to see if any more water is left and drain the excess again. Allow the substrate to cool for six hours.
2. Fill jars or polypropylene bags with the substrate, but do not overfill. Loosely put the jar's lid on or fold the bag over. Place in the pressure cooker and sterilize for two hours. Keep the substrate in the pressure cooker for six hours, allowing it to cool.
3. Gently crush and separate the spawn, but do not open the packet. Ensure your hands are clean before taking the substrate out of the pressure cooker. Add spawn to the substrate and seal the jars or bags. Shake to allow the spawn to mix into the substrate.
4. Keep in a room away from direct sunlight and a temperature between 18-25 degrees Celsius for three weeks. The substrate should be colonized and covered in white fungi. Move to an airy room and poke holes in the jar's lid or plastic. If you do not have high humidity, place jars or bags in a waterproof container and partially cover the top. Spray substrate twice a day to keep it moist but not wet.
5. A few weeks after moving rooms, the lion's mane will have grown through the holes, and they will be ready for harvesting.

Here are some tips and tricks to consider when growing your own lion's mane mushrooms:

- Substrate matters. Lion's mane mushrooms grow the best in hardwood substrate with about 10-20% supplemented with wheat bran.
- Although lion's mane does not need direct light, they require bright indirect light—the brighter and more natural the light, the better.
- Fewer holes mean bigger mushrooms, while more holes produce smaller mushrooms in higher quantities.

Growing Lion's Mane on Logs

Growing lion's mane mushrooms on logs is a great way to have a reliable and steady supply that will last for years. When using the growing bags as in the last method, you will have to go through replanting more often.

Materials needed to grow lion's mane on logs:

- lion mane's spawn plugs
- sealing wax
- hardwood logs

Equipment needed to grow lion's mane mushrooms on logs includes a hammer, drill, and small brush or paintbrush.

Follow these steps to grow your lion's mane on logs:

1. Buy lion's mane spawn plugs and logs. For a four-foot log, you will want about 30 to 50 plugs. A formula for determining how many plugs you will need is as follows: (length of log in centimeters x diameter of the log in centimeters) / 60.
2. Drill holes into the log six inches apart and an inch deep. Create rows and make sure to stagger them.
3. Insert lion's mane spawn plug dowels using a hammer to push them in gently. The spawn should be below the bark and flush with the wood.
4. Use melted sealing wax such as cheese wax to seal the holes.
5. Store logs in a shady place.
6. Water once or twice a week for ten minutes.
7. 12-18 months after planting your plugs, they will start to grow. When you begin to see the mushrooms grow, mist the logs daily and remove slugs if they begin to gather.
8. It can be as little as two weeks after your

Mushrooms start to fruit that you can harvest your delicious lion's mane.

How to Harvest Lion's Mane

The lion's mane mushroom is in a ball shape when ready to be harvested. Make sure you are delicately handling the mushroom while harvesting to prevent damage. Damage to the mushroom will make it go bad faster. Harvest your lion's mane mushroom by taking a knife and cutting the ball shape off close to the base where it is attached.

Depending on the type of texture you want from your mushrooms, you will pick your mushrooms at different times. Younger lion's mane will have a denser and firmer texture than older ones. Your lion's mane is ready for harvesting when the size of the ball stops growing in size, and the spines on it begin to grow longer and thicker. Immediately when this happens, you will want to harvest your mushroom for a firmer or denser texture. If you want a softer texture, you will wait longer to harvest.

How to Store and Clean Lion's Mane

Lion's mane mushrooms do not need to be processed immediately after you have harvested them. You can keep them stored in your refrigerator for up to a week.

To store your fresh lion's mane mushrooms, make sure you do not put them in your produce drawers. These mushrooms need good airflow so that they do not go bad. You can store your harvested mushrooms in a ventilated container or a paper bag. Do not wrap them tightly as it will reduce airflow.

If you cannot use all your mushrooms within the week, you can dry them and use them later. The uses for dried lion's mane mushrooms will differ from fresh ones. To dry your lion's mane mushroom, use the oven at a low temperature or a dehydrator if you have one. Make sure to chop the mushroom beforehand for a faster drying time.

Clean your lion's mane mushrooms similarly to reishi mushrooms. Give a quick rinse to remove any dirt and debris but do not submerge them in water, or they can go soggy.

How to Cook Lion's Mane Mushrooms

Studies of rats consuming lion's mane mushrooms showed no adverse reactions even when consuming a large quantity. The lion's mane mushroom is excellent for cooking and can be used for medicinal uses or to add some nutrients to your diet. However, if you have had allergic reactions to other species of mushrooms or have some form of sensitivity; it is best to avoid consuming this or any mushroom.

There are arious ways to cook lion's mane mushrooms, but one of the best universal methods is to pan-fry them. Pan-frying your fresh lion's mane mushrooms allows you to add them to various dishes, including sandwiches, stir fry, salads, or even eat it as a side dish.

To pan fpan-fry lion's mane mushrooms, follow these steps:

1. Cut mushrooms into slices, removing any dirty ends.
2. Use your choice of oil or butter and warm the skillet to medium heat.
3. Toss mushrooms in your seasoning of choice.
4. Cook for two minutes before flipping and cooking for another one or two minutes.
5. Serve and enjoy.

You can change up the seasoning of your choice to better suit the dish you are making. You can also create a sauce to toss them into.

Dried lion's mane can be used to create a powder to add to soups and stews to boost nutrients and flavor.

You can also use dried lion's mane to make tea or tinctures.

In the next chapter, we will explore another mushroom known as the "king of mushrooms" for its exceptional anti-inflammatory properties and helping people look younger from the inside out.

4

HOW TO LOOK YOUNG WITH CHAGA MUSHROOMS

The Chaga mushroom is considered the "king of mushrooms" because of the wide variety of uses we can get from them and the fantastic benefits we get from eating them. Chaga mushrooms get the name, "king of the mushrooms" because of the number of antioxidants they have and the effect this has on oxidative stress, which has been linked to aging and its ability to fight cancer. All the health benefits of the Chaga mushroom allow it to have age-defying benefits as it not only makes us feel younger, it can make us look younger.

Before we talk about the health benefits, a few people should avoid consuming Chaga. Depending on health conditions or medications that someone might be one, you should avoid consuming Chaga if you fit into any of the following categories:

- **Have kidney issues or are on dialysis.** Chaga mushrooms are full of oxalates. Oxalates are a compound in the body that forms crystals through binding calcium. These crystals can then impact bladder and kidney functions which is detrimental for anyone with preexisting kidney issues.
- **Are pregnant or breastfeeding.** No research has been done to see how consuming Chaga would impact an unborn child or breastfeeding infants, so it is best to avoid eating it.
- **About to have surgery or are on blood thinners.** Chaga mushrooms reduce blood clotting, which is essential for someone about to have surgery or on blood thinners.
- **Taking diabetic medications.** Chaga mushrooms can reduce blood sugar levels; however, they can interact negatively with diabetic medicine.
- **Have bone diseases such as osteoporosis.** Chaga mushrooms contain a compound known as calcium chelators which bind and remove calcium from the body. Calcium is essential for

people with bone diseases; thus, eating Chaga mushrooms could be dangerous.
- **Have been diagnosed with an autoimmune disease.** Chaga mushrooms are anti-inflammatory and can reduce immune function, but for those diagnosed with an autoimmune disease, when the body attacks itself, it can cause symptoms to worsen.

While some say that age is just a number, you can embody this by eating more Chaga and getting all the anti-aging benefits you want.

HEALTH BENEFITS

Research on the effects of Chaga mushrooms and many other species of fungi and mushrooms is still ongoing, with more human trials needed. However, preliminary studies show the massive impact that Chaga mushrooms can have on our health.

Combats Oxidative Stress

As we have discussed in other chapters, oxidative stress occurs when there is an imbalance between the antioxidants and free radicals. Antioxidants are needed to neutralize free radicals as they give an electron to a radical, making them less reactive and bringing balance back to the body. After a free radical has been given an electron, it helps fight off infection-causing pathogens, but when there are too many free radicals, it causes an imbalance and makes us more prone to infections.

When the body is under a state of oxidative stress, free radicals start to damage the body, including DNA, fatty tissues, and proteins. The damage caused by free radicals can result in numerous health concerns, including:

- inflammatory conditions
- cancer
- heart disease
- diabetes
- high blood pressure
- atherosclerosis, a condition that causes the blood vessels to harden
- neurodegenerative diseases

Oxidative stress does not only show up when we develop these dangerous health conditions; rather, it can show up first through signs of early aging, especially in the skin.

Everyone has free radicals flowing in them, but various factors might cause an increase in them. External factors that can increase free radicals include cigarette smoke, pollution, radiation, ozone, cleaners, and pesticides. A poor diet such as the one that is high in fat, sugar, and alcohol will also increase free radicals.

Chronic inflammation can lead to some of the same diseases as oxidative stress, including heart disease and rheumatoid arthritis. As oxidative stress increases the risk of many health issues, chronic inflammation is often a symptom of being under oxidative stress. In studies, the Chaga mushroom has been shown to help fight inflammation.

The immune system has various proteins and compounds to battle illness and diseases. The Chaga mushroom has been shown to increase one of these vital proteins known as cytokines. These proteins help regulate the immune system, telling it when to turn on and off. Chaga mushrooms have also been shown to stimulate white blood cells. The stimulation of white blood cells helps fight bacteria and viruses (Brown, 2018).

The body produces two types of cytokines, much like other proteins and compounds; beneficial and harmful cytokines. Chaga mushrooms increase the production of beneficial cytokines. It has also been shown to prevent the production of harmful ones responsible for keeping inflammation triggered and causing diseases.

One study on mice showed a decrease in inflammation and gut damage associated with it by preventing the production of harmful cytokines (Brown, 2018).

May Prevent the Growth and Formations of Cancer

Cancer is one of the leading causes of death worldwide, but luckily, many of the mushrooms that we have talked about can help prevent cancer and slow the growth of cancer. Some of the treatments that we use today use some form of mushroom or fungi or are derived from them. The strongest proof that mushrooms and fungi can prevent and slow the formation of cancer comes from test tubes and animal studies. More human studies still need to be conducted, but what has been done so far has had promising results.

Cancerous mice were shown to have a 60% reduction in tumor sizes after taking Chaga supplements. This reduction was further demonstrated in human cells during test-tube studies (Brown, 2018). Specifically, these studies have shown that Chaga mushrooms work strongest against colon, lung, prostate, and breast cancer cells.

Chaga mushrooms have some of the highest concentrates of antioxidants. When consumed, it helps balance free radicals, as we have talked about, and protect cells from any free radicals that do not become neutralized.

Specifically, the antioxidant triterpene is effective against killing cancer cells (Brown, 2018). More studies are needed to understand where the anti-cancer effects of Chaga mushrooms come from, but it is assumed to be linked to the high antioxidant levels.

Lowers Cholesterol

The word cholesterol typically has a negative connotation, but there are two types: good and bad. High-density lipoprotein (HDL) is known as good cholesterol, and it serves to absorb low-density lipoprotein (LDL) and bring it back to the liver so that it can be flushed from the body. When someone has a high LDL compared to HDL, they are more prone to heart disease.

Chaga extract has been shown to reduce LDL and increase HDL in an eight-week study on rats. The Chaga mushroom was also shown to increase the amount of antioxidants as it removed LDL and triglycerides (Brown, 2018). Multiple studies have shown the same results, giving strong evidence that it would have a similar effect on humans. Although there is no concrete answer, it is believed that the high number of antioxidants in Chaga is responsible for its ability to lower cholesterol.

HOW TO GROW CHAGA AT HOME

Growing Chaga at home is very difficult for numerous reasons. First, the part we harvest from Chaga does not contain spores as it is not the fruiting body, so we cannot plant pieces of Chaga to grow more mushrooms. Chaga mushrooms are parasitic and start growing as their spores attach to trees with a wound, which is the spot the Chaga mushroom forms.

You can cut into the trunk to create a wound if you have birch trees, and Chaga spores might latch on. But that is not guaranteed, and it is problematic. Because Chaga mushrooms are parasitic, any tree infested with them will eventually die. Yes, it might be years down the line, but the tree will still die. The second problem with this is that it can take years for Chaga mushrooms to become established. Growing Chaga at home isn't like other mushrooms that will start to show and can be harvested relatively quickly. It's unrealistic and impractical to try and grow Chaga at home, especially if you don't own a plot of land with many birch trees.

How to Grow Chaga on Birch Trees

If there is no sign of Chaga in the area, you will need to buy Chaga dowels. Farmers can buy Chaga dowels, but it is unlikely that individuals wanting to plant a couple of Chaga would be able to grow them. This is why it's impractical to grow them from home.

To grow Chaga mushrooms, birch trees need to be at least ten years old and ten centimeters in diameter. If you have a plot of land with a birch tree population, consider growing Chaga mushrooms or inspecting the trees for any signs of Chaga mushrooms.

Each tree will get 4-6 four-centimeter holes, which the dowels will be inserted into. For sustainability, keep the holes closer to the ground so that the upper half of the tree could be used for something else down the line, such as paper or firewood.

It can take a few years for Chaga to start showing, and then you can begin harvesting your medicinal mushrooms.

How to Find and Identify Chaga Mushrooms

If you live in the northern hemisphere, especially in an area that experiences a lot of cold weather, then you might have seen a Chaga mushroom and never realized. Chaga mushrooms grow in cold areas of the northern hemisphere, including Russia, Canada, Northern Europe, and some areas of the United States. Chaga mushrooms have relatively no mushrooms that grow in the same area and are similar in appearance. Those that might be mistaken for Chaga are not poisonous, making Chaga mushrooms safe for harvesting in the wild.

When you are looking to harvest Chaga mushrooms, birch trees are your best bet at finding them. Chaga mushrooms almost exclusively grow on birch trees. Chaga mushrooms will grow anywhere on the trunk of a tree but are most likely to be a few feet up or higher. Some Chaga mushrooms might require you to climb to get to them to harvest.

Chaga mushrooms can be found all year round, but it's best to harvest during the fall and winter since they prefer the cold. Most of a birch tree's energy and nutrients are stored in Chaga mushrooms during the winter, while the tree holds most in the summer. This means that a Chaga harvested in the winter will have more nutrients and medicinal properties. Chaga is also likely to be larger in the winter than in the summer as they spend the summer growing and then becoming dormant. One more practical reason to harvest your Chaga in the winter is that they are easier to see in the winter. Seeing a large black protrusion on a tree is much easier in the winter when the trees have lost their leaves and there is snow than in the summer.

How to Harvest Chaga

When harvesting Chaga mushrooms, you want to be sure that you are doing so sustainably. This means that you are not taking the entire mushroom as this will strip away the mycelium and kill the fungus in the process. Ripping away the entire mushroom also damages the tree, which is unnecessary.

To harvest Chaga mushrooms sustainably, use a knife to cut the pieces you want. You should also aim for bigger mushrooms, even if you only cut a small portion. This gives the smaller mushrooms more time to grow. Make sure that the knife or ax that you use is sharp so that the cut is clean and does not do any necessary damage to the mushroom. When you harvest smaller pieces from multiple different Chaga mushrooms, it keeps the area flourishing and will allow you to return the next year and not have to worry about not finding the mushrooms you need to harvest.

The state of the tree is critical when harvesting Chaga. Never harvest a Chaga mushroom from a dead tree or one that looks like it is dying. The tree may be contaminated with other types of fungus, and this may be passed onto the Chaga mushroom, which could be deadly for humans. Even if there is no other fungus present, the Chaga mushroom depends on the tree for life, so when it begins to die, so does the Chaga. Eating dying mushrooms will not only give you the nutrients you need or want, but it can also make you sick.

If you are worried that the mushroom you have harvested is not Chaga, break it open, and if it's orange in color, it is Chaga. Fungi that look like Chaga, such as the meshima mushroom or the black knot fungus, are not orange on the inside.

How to Clean, Dry, and Store Chaga

Chaga mushrooms are very susceptible to mold, so if you use them fresh, you should use them the same day. You should also dry your mushrooms the same day after you harvest them. After harvesting your Chaga mushrooms, use a knife to cut away any bark. The light-colored portions of the mushroom are the least nutritious and can be peeled away with your fingertips. This part of the mushroom will have the texture of cork. If you are cooking with fresh Chaga, it's recommended that you remove this part for a better texture. Use a knife to remove any dirt and debris, and if you need to, use a damp towel to wipe away any dirt. You want to avoid wetting the mushroom too much, or it could start to mold, especially if you do not start drying them right away.

To dry your Chaga, cut into one-inch cubes. Serrated knives are the best as Chaga is hard and dry in texture. Once you have cut your Chaga into pieces, leave it in the sun for a few days to dry out. You can also use the oven by setting it to its lowest temperature. Your Chaga mushrooms are dried completely when they are crumbly when you pick them up.

After drying your Chaga, you can either store it in chunks or create a powder. To create a powder, you can grate the dried pieces or crush them with a mortar and pestle.

To store your Chaga, have an air-tight container even when purchasing dried or powdered Chaga mushrooms. To ensure that no moisture can get to the mixture, add an oxygen absorber or food-safe silica packet to the container. Store the container in a cool and dark place that is pretty constant in temperature. Temperature fluctuations can cause the Chaga to go bad, so the perfect spot would be in a cabinet away from direct light. When you store your Chaga properly, you can keep it for up to two years and still get its medical uses.

How to Choose the Best Chaga

If you are buying Chaga mushrooms or products, there are multiple things you need to take into account before deciding on what you are going to buy. Before buying Chaga mushrooms, you need to think about the potency, which significantly differs between suppliers. The potency between different types of Chaga will also vary even when they are from the same supplier.

When buying Chaga mushroom products, make sure you are reading the labels. Take the time to read the label thoroughly. The labels will tell you many things you need to know before you buy something, including the country it came from and if the product includes other mushrooms with it.

After reading the labels, ask if tests have been done on the product. If you are buying something online, you can search the website or description to see the kinds of research or testing that have been done. If the seller has done tests, it can prove the claims they are making on the product and provide reassurance that the product is true to what is being marketed.

This next precaution can be harder for those buying products online, but examine the color of Chaga powder. The color of Chaga powder will range from light orange to dark brown. Powder that is dark brown contains the outer layer of the mushroom, while light orange will not have this layer included in the powder. Which type you buy is entirely up to you.

There is a lack of standardization done on Chaga products, so the best bet to do when purchasing Chaga online or in-person is to buy organic. Organic Chaga products ensure that the Chaga was not in an area where pesticides have been used, and no chemicals were used during processing and cleaning. Organic does not automatically mean that the product will be pure. There are still chances that other products are mixed with it, and you will want to take the other steps to ensure it is the right product for you.

Different Types of Chaga

Although there is only one species of Chaga, it can be divided into three different parts. Products can be made from individual parts, so if you are looking for a product made with the whole mushroom or just one part, read the labels to see what it is made of. The first part of the mushroom is the outermost layer that is hard and dense and black in color. A fun fact is that the outer layer is black due to a large amount of melanin. The second part of the Chaga mushroom is considered the middle layer and is dark orange. This layer is dense but not nearly as much as the outer layer. The third part is the inner layer, which is light orange and has a texture similar to cork. This part can be peeled away. All three of these parts can be used for medicinal purposes, and often most products will use all three.

How to Make Chaga Tea

Chaga mushroom tea is one of the most common and best ways to consume all the nutrients, vitamins, and minerals from Chaga mushrooms. You can get some of the benefits from Chaga mushrooms by eating them as you would a regular mushroom, but it has been shown that extracting the nutrients by making tea, or by drying them and using a powder, will give you a lot more benefits as it helps to concentrate the vitamins and minerals.

To make Chaga tea, use the following steps:

1. Boil water on a stove before adding Chaga mushrooms. Using a kettle isn't recommended as the water will not stay hot long enough to allow for a proper extraction to occur.
2. Add Chaga mushrooms and allow them to simmer for 10-15 minutes. You can use fresh mushrooms that are sliced or cut into chunks, or you can use Chaga powder in your own tea bags and steep.

3. If you are using fresh Chaga, strain and enjoy your tea.

Chaga tea is best drunk while hot, and you can sweeten it with maple syrup, sugar, or honey. Your milk of choice can also be added if you desire.

The next mushroom might be one you hold close to your heart, and the benefits you get from it go hand in hand. In the next chapter, we will discuss a classic that you might not have known would give you amazing heart health benefits. The mushroom we will discuss in the next chapter is the shiitake mushroom.

5

SHIITAKE MUSHROOMS: GIVE YOUR HEART WHAT IT DESERVES

The heart is the life force of the body. With each pump it is sending blood and other essential compounds to other parts of the body. If we are going to start taking care of our bodies, we also have to take care of our hearts. Anything that affects our heart will affect everything, so it's essential to take care of it. The shiitake mushroom, a staple in many households and extremely easy to come about in grocery stores, has some fantastic heart health benefits that will give this hardworking organ the care it deserves and needs to keep us healthy and happy.

BENEFITS OF SHIITAKE

Although one of the most common mushrooms that you can buy in the store, shiitake mushrooms have a lot of benefits. Much like the other mushrooms we have talked about, this mushroom has immune-boosting abilities and anti-cancer properties. However, for the focus of this section, we will talk about the benefits that make the shiitake mushroom different from the other mushrooms and fungi that we have discussed so far in this book.

Boosts Heart Health

The biggest benefit you can get from eating shiitake mushrooms is boosting overall heart health. Unlike other mushrooms that will only lower cholesterol, the shiitake mushroom attacks heart health from multiple fronts. The shiitake mushroom has been shown to reduce bad cholesterol with three different compounds:

- *sterols:* help to block cholesterol absorption that occurs in the stomach
- *eritadenine:* inhibits the production of enzymes that produce cholesterol
- *beta-glucans:* a fiber that lowers cholesterol

Shiitakes mushrooms contain all three of these compounds, which helps lower cholesterol. Lowering cholesterol isn't the only way that shiitake mushrooms can help to boost heart health. Studies of rats showed that taking shiitake mushroom powder regulated blood pressure by preventing it from increasing (Jennings, 2019). Unfortunately, this study was done on rats with high blood pressure, so there is no way to tell the effects on rats with healthy blood pressure.

Further studies on rats showed the effect of including mushrooms on a high-fat diet. Both groups of rats were on the same high-fat diet, but one group was given shiitake mushrooms, and one was not. The group of rats given mushrooms showed reduced fat levels in the liver, lower cholesterol, and less plaque on the artery walls (Jennings, 2019). Regulating blood pressure, reducing plaque, and lowering cholesterol are all vital for improving circulation, which will boost heart health.

May Strengthen Bones

So far, none of the mushrooms have been said to help strengthen bones; however, all mushrooms have vitamin D, which is vital for bone strength. Depending on how mushrooms are grown, the vitamin D levels will fluctuate, but the vitamin D levels are improved when exposed to UV lights. Studies on mice compared two groups. The first was given a low-vitamin D and low calcium diet, and after some time, the mice started to develop osteoporosis symptoms. The second group was given the same diet but also given shiitake mushrooms, and had a higher bone density than the first (Jennings, 2019). The second group was given shiitake mushrooms grown with UV light, so it is unsure if regularly grown mushrooms would have the same effect. More studies would need to be done on humans to know if the mushrooms would have the same effect.

Promising Antiviral and Antibacterial Effects

The last benefit that we will talk about associated with shiitake mushrooms is the possible antiviral and antibacterial effects that one can get from them. The shiitake mushroom has various antifungal, antibacterial, and antiviral compounds. Living through a pandemic, illnesses and diseases have evolved to become more antibiotic-resistant even before this. New medications and antibiotics are needed to tackle this, and scientists are starting to turn to the shiitake mushroom. No animal or human studies have been conducted to look at these effects, but test-tube studies have started. Initial studies showed that eating shiitake mushrooms is likely not to have these benefits, but isolating the compounds can.

Possible Side Effects of Shiitake

According to studies and their availability on the market, Shiitakes are safe to eat. However, there have been some cases of side effects, but they are typically rare and associated with an allergic reaction. Some people develop rashes on their skin after handling or eating raw shiitake mushrooms. Other rare causes included sensitivity to sunlight and upset stomach after using powdered shiitake mushroom extract for an extended period of time.

HOW TO GROW SHIITAKE MUSHROOMS FOR JUST FIVE DOLL ARS

Growing your own medicinal mushrooms has multiple benefits, including saving money and giving you more access to medicinal mushrooms. You also know how the mushrooms are grown when you do it from home, so you do not need to worry about any pesticides or chemicals that might have been used during the growing and harvesting process. It is often believed that you need to have a lot of money to start a garden, but you can start growing your own shiitake mushrooms for as little as five dollars.

Materials and equipment you will need to grow shiitake mushrooms include:

- 100 or so inoculated shiitake mushroom lumps
- cheese wax, trade wax, or beeswax
- hardwood tree sections with the bark and two recent cut
- multipurpose drill
- paintbrush
- camping stove or heat source
- rubber mallet or hammer

This seems like you will need to buy a lot of things. But, the good news is, you can always ask to borrow many of the items, since you do not need to buy all new items to grow your shiitake mushrooms.

After you have collected all your materials and equipment, it is time to start growing your shiitake mushrooms. Use the following steps to do so:

1. **Cut sections of a hardwood tree.** Your pieces of hardwood should be about three to four feet long, be no smaller than four inches and no bigger than eight inches in diameter. Small sections are needed to allow the shiitake to grow.
2. **Purchase plugs online.** For 100 plugs, you will want to have two logs. Allow your mushroom plugs to rest for 15 days.
3. **Drill three to four-inch deep holes into the wood.** A three or four-foot log will hold about 50 plugs. The rows of holes should form a diamond pattern.
4. **Insert plugs into holes.** Clean your hands before inserting the plugs. Gently tap the plugs into each hole using a mallet or hammer.
5. **Melt wax and seal holes.** Use a cheap paint brush to brush melted wax over the holes, sealing them. If any holes do not have a plug, fill them with wax. Sealing the holes prevents other fungi from forming.

6. **Incubate for six to 12 months.** Store the logs in a shady and moist place. Cover with a breathable cloth if you wish. Water the logs every day, except during the winter. Watering in the winter can cause the plugs to die. Moisture in the storage area should be enough winter to support the logs.
7. **Initiate your mushrooms.** After nine to 10 months, it's time to initiate the mushrooms. During this process, you will submerge the logs in water for 24 hours. After submerging the logs, stand them upright in a shady area. Soon after the initiation process, shiitake mushrooms will start to grow, and you will be able to harvest them.

How to Harvest Shiitake Mushrooms

Shiitake mushrooms are great for home growers because they do not have a specific time to harvest them. Rather, it all depends on your personal preference about the size of fruit you want. Typically for cooking, you will want smaller shiitake fruit because it is more flavorful and has a more desirable texture than bigger and older fruits. Younger shiitake fruit has a longer shelf life, and if you are not growing on a commercial level, there is no need for the larger yield associated with letting the shiitake continue to grow.

Shiitake are relatively hardy and, when young, are less susceptible to damages, but you avoid manhandling them too much. Have a basket or bucket with you when harvesting so that the mushroom can sit instead of needing to be constantly handled. Take a knife and cut the mushroom from the stem to harvest your shiitake. Place the severed mushroom in the basket and harvest as many as you would like. The best type of day to harvest your mushrooms would be on a day where it is relatively dry. Shiitake that are young and allowed to dry before being put into the fridge can last up to two weeks in the fridge.

How to Store Shiitake Mushrooms

Shiitake mushrooms can last for about two weeks in a fridge below 4 degrees Celsius. Washing a shiitake mushroom before storing it in the refrigerator will only allow them to stay good for a couple of days. After buying or harvesting your shiitake mushrooms, do not clean or slice them unless you are using them the same or the next day. Wrap the shiitake in a paper bag or paper towels loosely. These mushrooms need airflow, so they should not be stored in the produce crispers of the fridge.

How to Clean and Cook Shiitake Mushrooms

Cleaning your shiitake mushrooms is a necessary step before cooking with them. Shiitakes, like other mushrooms, will absorb a lot of water, so be sure to give them a quick rinse with cold water but do not submerge them. Give your mushrooms a shake before patting them dry with a paper towel to help get rid of any excess water. Shiitakes should be mostly dry before cooking them but do not need to be completely dry.

Remove the stems, but wait to throw them out because they can still be useful after cutting them off. There will be some remnants of stem remaining after you have harvested them. Your shiitake stems can be put into a compost bin if you have one, or you can freeze them to use them in vegetable stock.

To cook evenly, cut the mushroom caps into strips or cubes. Leaving the cap intact can make it harder to cook.

Shiitake is often used as a substitute for meat because of the meaty flavor and the juicy and chewy texture it can have when cooked. How you cook shiitake mushrooms is entirely up to you. You can either combine them in other dishes or make them as a side dish. Common dishes that contain shiitake mushrooms include pasta with white or red sauce, noodles, stir fry, ramen, stews, soups, and avocado toast. These are only a handful of meals you can make with shiitake mushrooms.

Here is a Japanese-style recipe that will change how you look at shiitake mushrooms. For this recipe, you are going to need:

- one cup of sliced shiitake mushrooms
- two tablespoons of soy sauce
- one tablespoon of sesame oil

To prepare your shiitake mushrooms, follow this recipe:

1. Heat a non-stick skillet over medium heat.
2. Add sesame oil, soy sauce, and shiitake into the pan.
3. Sauté until shiitakes are soft, about three minutes

Serve these mushrooms any way you want, either by themselves or as part of a dish. This recipe is quick and easy, only taking a maximum of ten minutes to prepare.

There are always the stories of someone healthy their entire life being diagnosed with cancer. Even the most healthy individuals can develop cancer. There are also cases of people who do not have a healthy diet not developing any typical health concerns associated with a poor diet. This just shows that cancer and other diseases can get to anyone. This is why it is essential to take precautions and eat foods known for preventing cancer and other diseases from developing. In the next chapter, we will discuss a mushroom known for its anti-cancer properties, and that mushroom is the turkey tail.

6

FIGHT CANCER CELLS WITH TURKEY TAIL MUSHROOMS

No, turkey tail isn't a new cut of meat that you will be eating for Thanksgiving dinner. It is a mushroom renowned for its health benefits, and you might want to consider adding it to your plate. The nutrients that we consume daily serve to be our defense against cancer. When we don't have enough nutrients, the body's warriors, the white blood cells, the natural killer cells, and many other proteins and compounds cannot fight off diseases and viruses, and our body would become overwhelmed. Even the healthiest individuals can have their bodies falling victim to disease and illness. However, eating more foods rich in essential nutrients such as the turkey tail mushroom will prevent these diseases from forming and growing if they do enter the body.

IMMUNE BOOSTING BENEFITS

The cancer-fighting properties of the turkey tail mushroom come from all its immune-boosting properties. Many medicinal mushrooms have some of these benefits, but what makes the turkey tail mushroom one of the most researched mushrooms for its cancer-fighting and immune-boosting properties. While another mushroom might have one or two immune-boosting abilities, the turkey tail has five.

Improve Immune Function in Cancer Patients

Test-tube studies of the turkey tail mushrooms have shown antitumor properties that help stop the growth and spread of tumors. The reduction in tumor size has been connected to the turkey tail mushroom's ability to boost immune function.

Specific studies showed that dogs diagnosed with hemangiosarcoma, an aggressive form of cancer, who were given 45.5 milligrams of turkey mushroom extract per pound of their body weight a day saw significant reductions in the spread and growth of cancer cells (Kubala, 2018). Turkey tail mushrooms have been successfully used alongside radiation and chemotherapy treatments for humans.

Enhance the Speed of Cancer Treatments

After years of medical trials and research, turkey tail mushrooms are among the most widely used mushrooms for treating cancer alongside traditional treatments such as chemotherapy. Studies showed that by combining chemotherapy with herbal remedies such as the turkey tail mushroom, there was a significant increase in survival rates. An analysis of gastric, breast, and rectal cancer patients showed that those treated with both turkey tail and chemotherapy saw a 9% reduction in mortality than those that did not (Kubala, 2018).

Another study of breast cancer patients also showed an increase in cancer-fighting cells such as lymphocytes and natural killer cells in patients given turkey tail powder daily. These patients were given around 6-9 grams of dried turkey tail powder (Kubala, 2018).

Chock-Full of Polysaccharopeptides

Polysaccharopeptides are potent immune-boosting compounds, and turkey tail mushrooms are chock-full of them. Polysaccharide (PSP) and Krestin (PSK) Peptides are two of the best polysaccharopeptides that someone can have, and both are found in turkey tail mushrooms. Both of these compounds can activate and inhibit immune cells. One of the cells can trigger the immune system to create more natural killer cells to help fight cancer.

Test-tube studies of PSP showed that it activates monocyte activity (Kubala, 2018). Monocytes are white blood cells that boost immunity and fight infections. PSK activates white blood cells known as macrophages which are protectors. They are meant to protect the body from harmful bacteria and substances. PSK also activates dendritic cells. These cells help regulate the responses of our immune system and promote immunity against toxins.

Turkey tail extracts will be used during surgery, radiation, and chemotherapy because of the immune-boosting powers that PSP and PSK have. Those undergoing surgery or who have cancer are more prone to infections, so the PSK and PSP in turkey tail help bring the immune system back up.

Packed with Antioxidants

Oxidative stress is one of the leading factors of chronic inflammation and cancer. Oxidative stress causes damage to the cells, which can lead to the development of health conditions such as cancer and heart disease. Antioxidants help stabilize free radicals, which relieve oxidative stress and stop the cellular damage and inflammation they cause.

Turkey tail contains phenols and flavonoids, both antioxidants which reduce inflammation and increase the production and release of protective compounds. These protective compounds include quercetin which releases "immunoprotective proteins like interferon-y, while inhibiting the release of the pro-inflammatory enzymes cyclooxygenase (COX) and lipoxygenase (LOX)" (Kubala, 2018).

Can Improve Gut Health

A healthy gut promotes a healthy immune system. The bacteria in our gut interacts with the cells of our immune system, and when our gut bacteria is not healthy, it negatively impacts our immune systems. Prebiotics help increase healthy gut bacteria, and turkey tail mushrooms contain significant levels of prebiotics.

A study of 24 people over eight weeks showed an increase in beneficial gut bacteria and a reduction of harmful bacteria such as E. coli when they consumed 3,600 milligrams of turkey tail extracted PSP (Kubala, 2018). Turkey tail mushrooms increase healthy bacteria such as bifidobacterium and lactobacillus, which help to improve intestinal symptoms and digestion, reduce cholesterol, enhance immune system function, and lower the risk of developing cancers.

POTENTIAL RISKS

Turkey tails are associated with minimal side effects. The most common side effects people get from consuming turkey tail include bloating, gas, and dark stools. An extremely rare side effect that was reported was the darkening of fingernails.

Turkey tail is one of the most used mushrooms for cancer treatments and is often used alongside chemotherapy. Symptoms such as loss of appetite, nausea, and vomiting have been seen while cancer patients were under treatment. Still, it could not be determined if the turkey tail mushrooms were responsible for these symptoms along with the chemotherapy treatment.

Before starting any new supplement, be sure to talk to your doctor to ensure the supplement will not interfere with any medication you might be taking or underlying conditions you have.

HOW TO GROW TURKEY TAIL MUSHROOMS

Growing your own turkey tail mushroom is a great way to ensure you get all the anti-cancer properties you need. Growing your own mushrooms, such as turkey tails, are a great way to make a small income. Depending on how much you use your turkey tail and how much you have, you can sell some to neighbors, friends, or family and make some money from the little bit of turkey tail mushrooms you have.

To grow turkey tail mushrooms, you are going to need:

- Log or stump of hardwood such as maple, oak, and pine. If you choose a log that is around three to eight inches long. Stumps are a lot easier to grow turkey mushrooms on than logs.

- drill with 5/16 inch bit
- turkey tail spawn plugs
- hammer or rubber mallet
- cheese wax or beeswax
- rubbing alcohol to sterilize
- paintbrush

Follow these steps to grow your own turkey tail mushrooms at home:

1. After choosing your log or stump to grow, sterilize your 5/16 inch bit and drill holes about 1 1/4 inch deep.
2. Drill holes four inches apart in staggered rows on the stump or log.
3. Insert the plugs into the holes, gently hammering them down into place.
4. Melt wax and brush it over the plug-filled holes to seal them. Also, fill any empty holes with wax to stop any insects or other mushrooms from forming.
5. Keep the logs or stump in a shaded spot.
6. Give stumps about 1-2 inches of water a week and a little more to logs. Stumps will use their

roots to help water the mushrooms. Logs might require more water.
7. It will take almost a year for mushrooms to start growing, and then you can harvest them and do with them as you wish.

Types of Turkey Tail Mushrooms

Turkey tails can often be complicated for beginners because three different scientific names know them; however, they all refer to the same type of mushroom. Depending on the climate and the wood the mushroom is growing on, the color, shape, and size might differ slightly, but they are all the same species of mushroom.

How to Identify Turkey Tail Mushrooms

Turkey tail mushrooms are located worldwide, including Asia, North America, central Europe, Britain, and Ireland. These mushrooms grow on dead hardwood trees, stumps, and branches, growing all year round. Turkey tail mushrooms will differ in shape and size depending on the species. Some are more muted in color, while others are vividly colored. A single turkey tail is made up of multiple layered caps that will be between one and three millimeters thick. The caps will be flat or convex, depending on the maturity of the mushroom.

The turkey tail is easy to identify by the concentric rings on each cap. The colors of the turkey tail will follow this ring pattern. The most common colors that turkey tail mushrooms will take on include white, red, brown, orange, and gray. But because the colors of these mushrooms differ so much, color should be your last mode of identifying turkey tails.

The underside of a turkey tail mushroom ranges from white to light brown and is covered in pores. This is where the spores of the mushrooms are released. The pores of a turkey tail mushroom are tiny and often require us to squint to see them.

The turkey tail mushrooms have such a distinct look that often, the only lookalikes you will find are other species of turkey tail. None of these lookalikes are poisonous, with the worst-case scenario being that the mushroom might have an unpleasant taste. Not all turkey tail species have the same range of medicinal properties either.

Commonly, people will mistake trametes mushrooms with turkey tails, and although they are part of the same family, they are not the same. These mushrooms will generally be grayer and will not have the colored bands of a turkey tail mushroom. The underside is also different as they will have larger and fewer pores than turkey mushrooms.

Other mushrooms commonly mistaken for the turkey tail include stereum ostrea, trichaptum abietinum, and lenzites betulina. All three of these species have caps that look similar to turkey tails, but their undersides reveal they are not, as they do not have the white or light brown underside with pores.

How to Harvest Turkey Tail Mushrooms

To harvest turkey tail mushrooms, you will need your hands and a knife. Small turkey tails will be able to be twisted off the tree with your hands, but larger ones will require a knife to help separate the mushroom from the tree. Before harvesting your mushrooms, look for any signs that insects have been eating the mush-room. Also, look for any signs of mold or imperfections on the mushroom. The mushroom size does not reflect the medicinal properties it has.

How to Clean Turkey Tail Mushrooms

Turkey tails grow on trees, both living and dead, and are unlikely to have a lot of dirt on them. All the same, you still need to be looking for signs of molds, insects, or other problems that the mushroom might have. If you are harvesting turkey tail mushrooms from dead trees, you really need to be looking for any mold or insects that might have caused the tree to die and have been passed on to the mushroom.

After inspecting the mushroom for any mold or insects, take a soft toothbrush to brush away the dirt or debris on the mushroom gently. The part of the turkey tail attached to the tree will have the most debris, and you can either try to remove all the debris or cut this part of the mushroom off. If the mushroom is extremely dirty for some reason, you can give it a quick rinse, but do not submerge the mushroom as it will absorb the water.

How to Dry and Store Turkey Tail Mushrooms

Turkey tail mushrooms do not last long after being removed from the tree. Drying them immediately after harvesting them is your best option so that the mushrooms do not start to mold. Turkey mushrooms are very tough, to the point that many deem them inedible; however, drying them is a great option. Dry turkey mushrooms in a food dehydrator or set the oven to the lowest setting. Cut your mushrooms into one-inch chunks or slices to allow them to dry easier. After you have dried them, you can either store them as they are or turn them into a food powder in a food processor or mortar and pestle.

Once you have dried your turkey mushroom, you can store it for a very long time as long as it is stored in an air-tight container and a cool and dark place. However, if you will store turkey tail mushroom powder or chunks for longer than a few months, make sure you add food-safe silica packs or oxygen absorbers to absorb any moisture and keep the product from going stale or stale bad.

How to Cook and Make Turkey Tail Tea

The texture of the turkey tail is not the most desirable; you are not going to cook it and serve it like you would a shiitake mushroom. Rather, you will use the turkey tail powder that you used to add to dishes such as soups, stews, or smoothies to get an extra dose of nutri-ents. Using the dried turkey tail in this way is only one option. Another option is to make turkey tail tea.

You can make this tea with fresh or dried turkey tail, but the steps will differ slightly. To make fresh turkey tail mushroom tea, follow these steps:

1. Boil five cups of water on the stove.
2. Chop up one cup of turkey tail and add to boiling water.
3. Boil for at least one hour.
4. After boiling, most of the water would have evaporated, and you are left with a concentrated tea.
5. Strain out the chunks of turkey tail and enjoy.

You can also make turkey tail tea with powder or dried chunks and prepare it as you would with any tea. Boil water, allow it to steep for a few minutes, and enjoy. You can sweeten your tea with honey or add milk if you desire.

The next mushroom we will talk about is known for boosting athleticism and increasing energy, which is ironic, as its nickname is the zombie mushroom. All the immune-boosting benefits we can get from turkey tail mushrooms are amazing—and knowing that you can have access to these mushrooms regularly can ease a lot of anxiety you might have about health. Keep reading to find out everything about cordyceps.

7

CORDYCEPS MUSHROOM: YOUR ENERGY BOOSTER

For many individuals, fatigue is an everyday experience, and it makes it very hard to do heavier tasks or even get through the day. Although this is a regular occurrence for many people, it doesn't mean that it is healthy. There are various ways to increase your energy levels, including practicing healthy habits such as exercise and sleeping regularly. Even when practicing these healthy habits, though, sometimes we need an energy booster to get through the day. Cordyceps are a natural energy booster you can utilize while also getting many medicinal benefits.

Cordyceps, also known as zombie mushrooms, Chinese caterpillar fungus, and vegetable caterpillar, is a fungus species that inhabit the high mountain ranges of China and Tibet. This fungus will grow by having its spores infest caterpillar larvae and will continue to grow as the caterpillar does. Eventually, the caterpillar will die, and the fungus will continue to grow until long tendrils escape the caterpillar. Cordyceps have been used as part of traditional Chinese medicine for centuries, dating back to 5000 B.C. There is a folktale that they were discovered in 500 A.D. when yak herbers noticed their yaks being unnaturally energetic, and it was said that they ate some cordyceps as they were grazing.

According to Chinese medicinal records, the uses of cordyceps have changed over time and differ based on who is using them. Tibetan shamans were said to drink cordyceps tea before climbing the mountain because it made the climb easier on them. In comparison, healers in India used cordyceps to treat various issues, including tuberculosis, asthma, cancer, the common cold, hepatitis, diabetes, and erectile dysfunction.

There are 350 known species when discussing cordyceps, but only two have really been researched and used actively. The first species of cordyceps is c. sinensis, and the second is c. militaris. **C. sinensis** is a species that grows in caterpillars in the mountains. These fungi are now incredibly rare and come with a hefty price because of this rarity and thus are not often used in the supplements that people can buy. **C. militaris** has the same properties as the former but is a species that can be commercially cultivated and is grown on rice. Because this can be grown and cultivated in masses large enough for the demand and has the same benefits as c. sinensis, it is affordable and accessible for anyone wanting to try cordyceps.

C. sinensis has such beneficial properties that they were given the status of being a herbal drug in 1964. Only this species of cordyceps has this status. However, the environment of the *c. sinensis*, specifically in the Tibetan mountains, has fallen victim to over-exploration, which is why *C. militaris* has taken over as being the primary cordyceps used and sold.

BENEFITS OF CORDYCEPS

Cordyceps have a long history of use and plenty of research to back it up. There were also athletic scandals that involved cordyceps. In the 1990s, the Chinese Olympic women's running team attributed their success to using cordyceps to boost their athletic abili- ties. However, it was later proven that they were using drugs to enhance their performance; their claims of cordyceps raising their athletic abilities hold some merit.

Boost Athletic Performance

Cordyceps can improve our athletic performance in multiple ways. The first way that cordyceps help to boost our athletic performances is by increasing our resistance to fatigue. The energy-boosting properties that you might want from this fungus will come from this ability. More studies are needed in humans to see the extent of the fatigue resistance from this fungus. A study conducted in 2015 on mice showed that c. mili-taris effectively relieves fatigue and increases our fatigue resistance (Sheilds, n.d.).

The second way cordyceps can boost athletic performance is by increasing our V02 max levels. V02 max is the measurement of how much oxygen is consumed during high-intensity workouts. Specialists will use this measurement to determine someone's fitness level. A study conducted on a group of healthy adults showed an increase in V02 max by 7%. This study looked at two groups, one given a placebo and the other given cordyceps. Those given placebos saw no increase, while those with the cordyceps saw a 7% increase (Van De Walle, 2018). However, this study did not look at how cordyceps would affect highly trained athletes. The people who participated were average fitness levels and were given around 3 grams of cordy-ceps a day. It is assumed that athletes would need to take a higher dose of cordyceps to see an increase in their V02 max.

The third way cordyceps help improve athletic performance is by increasing the production of ATP (adenosine triphosphate), a compound that carries energy throughout the body. Increasing this production allows cordyceps to boost a person's V02 max levels and fatigue resistance. However, more studies need to be done to determine if this increase occurs during exercise or not.

Anti-Aging Properties

Anti-aging is often only thought of regarding our appearance, but multiple changes occur, including becoming more fatigued, having a lower sex drive, memory issues, and decreasing strength. Studies of mice showed improved sexual function and memory (Van De Walle, 2018). Antioxidants in cordyceps help neutralize free radicals, which we know is a leading cause of early aging and increased risk of diseases.

Another recent study revealed that fruit flies that ate cordyceps had an extended life to those that didn't (Van De Walle, 2018). Although fruit flies are very far from humans, this discovery is the first to reveal what significant anti-aging properties might come from consuming cordyceps.

Can Help Manage Type 2 Diabetes

Insulin is a product used to help people with diabetes regulate their blood sugar levels. Cordyceps contains a type of sugar that mimics the effects of insulin, thus helping to manage blood sugar levels and symptoms associated with Type 2 diabetes. Studies on mice have also shown that cordyceps might have the ability to decrease blood sugar levels and might protect against kidney disease, a complication common in people with diabetes. A study on people diagnosed with chronic kidney disease showed improved kidney function after taking cordyceps supplements (Van De Walle, 2018).

Has Potential Anti-Tumor Effects

As we know, turkey tails are one mushroom used for the anti-cancer and anti-tumor properties, and cordyceps have been under many studies for the potential anti-tumor effects. Human studies have not been conducted by test-tube, and animal studies have given some preliminary evidence that is positive for humans having similar responses.

Cordyceps inhibited the growth of various types of cancer in human cells, including colon, liver, lung, and skin. Studies in mice also showed cordyceps had anti- tumor effects on lung cancer, lymphoma, and melanoma (Van De Walle, 2018).

Cordyceps have also been shown to help relieve the side effects of some cancer treatments, including radiation and chemotherapy. Leukopenia, a common side effect of cancer treatments, was reversed when people consumed cordyceps.

HOW TO GROW CORDYCEPS MUSHROOMS

Cordyceps are not cultivated worldwide like oyster or shiitake mushrooms because they are very labor-intensive and have a high labor cost. A few companies are starting to get cultivation off the ground in the United States, but it is still in the very early stages and will not be grown commercially for a while longer. However, growing cordyceps from home is a perfectly viable option and allows you to access all the benefits from cordyceps. Obviously, we will not be growing the c. sinensis species, but one similar to the c. militaris.

Materials and equipment needed to grow cordyceps include:

- Large mixing bowl
- Measuring cups and spoons
- 72 pint jars
- 1 gallon of water
- 2 tablespoons of rice per jar (144 tablespoons total)
- 1/2 cup of starch
- 1/4 cup of nutritional yeast
- 5 scoops of baby food
- 2 tablespoons of azomite
- 2 tablespoons of sugar

Follow these steps to grow your own cordyceps:

1. Add two tablespoons of rice into each jar.
2. Combine water, starch, yeast, baby food (powdered), azomite, and sugar in a large mixing bowl. Mix until all the ingredients have dissolved. In each jar, add 1/4 cup of the liquid mixture.
3. Seal the jar tightly.

4. Add cordyceps spawn or wedges from petri plates that are grown in labs.
5. Keep in a well-ventilated area so that air-born contaminants cannot infect the dishes.
6. Keep in a dark area between 55-75 degrees Fahrenheit. The mycelium cordyceps will start to grow rather quickly, and at about 21 days, the jar will be fully colonized.
7. After colonization, it is time to fruit the cordyceps. These fungi grow towards the light, so if you are growing the cordyceps on shelves, have a light source on every shelf. You will want to have the jar exposed to 16 hours of light and 8 hours in the dark for the best results. Keep the temperature around 60-70 degrees Fahrenheit for fruiting.
8. Keep the jars sealed. This helps to maintain moisture and oxygen levels so that you do not need to manage these levels and risk killing the fruiting fungus.

How to Harvest Cordyceps

Your cordyceps will take about 4-6 weeks to fruit and require little maintenance. These fungi can continue to grow until they reach the top of the jar, but not all of them will reach this height. Harvest your cordyceps when they reach the top, or they have stopped growing.

If most of your cordyceps have been harvested, but some are not that tall, harvest them anyway since they are likely done growing and won't ever reach the top of the jar.

The great thing about cordyceps is that you can use both the fruiting body and the grain medium used to colonize. The grain medium can be used to extract medicinal properties as it acts like the mycelium of the fungus. The grain medium can also be made into a tempeh dish. To harvest the fruiting bodies, pluck them from the substrate and grain medium. Unlike other fungi and mushrooms, cordyceps only have one life cycle, so there is no root system to worry about.

If you have bought cordyceps growing kits, be sure to read the instructions, if any, about how to harvest the cordyceps.

How to Clean Cordyceps

When using fresh cordyceps, it is very important to make sure they are clean. They need to be cleaned thor-oughly whether they were made in a grain medium or are *C. sinensis* and used larvae to grow. Clean your cordyceps with a toothbrush or rinse with water to remove any debris that is on them. If you are using water, do not submerge them; rather, use a colander to rinse them and allow the water to drain simultaneously.

How to Cook Cordyceps Mushrooms

Cooking with cordyceps is a great way to make delicious healthy meals while also getting all their benefits. Cooking cordyceps with water is one of the most common and easiest ways to cook them. It is as simple as adding cordyceps to a cup of water and cooking for 10 minutes, The cordyceps could then be eaten and the water used to drink or for cooking.

Another very common use of cordyceps is to make a stew with them; however, you will add in the cordyceps later. You do not want to have the cordyceps inside the stew as it cooks for a long time as it can lose all the nutrients, signified when the cordyceps start to turn white. Add the fungi in the last half hour of the stew cooking and then enjoy them.

Another way to use your cordyceps is to dry them and grind them into powder. Dry them using the oven food dehydrator, or leave them in the sun. After the cordyceps are completely dry, use a mortar, pestle, or food processor to create a powder. Store in an air-tight container and add a food-safe silica packet or oxygen absorber to keep the powder from becoming moist. Having your cordyceps turned into a powder is a great way to get the nutrients and health benefits of the cordyceps without needing to cook them.

Three Cordyceps Recipes to Try

Here are three cordyceps recipes to try if you want to test out how you can intercorporate cordyceps into your meals.

Cordyceps Soup

Ingredients:

- 8 cups of water
- 4 sliced red dates
- 4 dried mushrooms of choice
- a handful of fresh or dried, whole cordyceps
- 1/2 teaspoon of salt
- Soup ingredients of choice. For example, if you want to make chicken soup, add the ingredients for chicken soup.
- optional: chopped sweet corn and carrots, or any other vegetable of choice

Instructions:

1. Bring 8 cups of water to a boil.
2. Add cordyceps, dates, mushrooms, salt, and any other soup ingredients you would like.
3. Cover pot and reduce heat to medium. Allow to simmer for two hours.

4. Ensure that the vegetables are tender. Serve hot and enjoy.

Poached Cordyceps

Ingredients:

- 30 grams of cordyceps
- Salt, sesame oil, sugar, and Sichuan pepper oil to taste.

Instructions:

1. Soak cordyceps in cold water for five minutes.
2. Fill a skillet half full with water and bring to boil.
3. Strain cordyceps and place them into a skillet.
4. Poach for 30 seconds, stirring the cordyceps.
5. Strain and dunk into a cold water bowl.
6. After dunking them, you can throw them into a hot pan with your seasoning to serve hot. Or you can mix the seasonings in a bowl and toss the cordyceps, serving them chilled.

Cordyceps and Pasta

Ingredients:

- 3 ounces of spaghetti of choice
- 60 grams of cordyceps
- 60 milliliters of white wine
- 30 milliliters of oil
- one chopped shallot or small onion
- optional: 90 milliliters of dashi
- spaghetti sauce of choice

Instructions:

1. Cook spaghetti by the directions of the packet.
2. Heat the skillet over medium heat and add oil. Chop shallot or onion and add to the oil. Cook for about three minutes or until it becomes fragrant.
3. Add white wine to the skillet and stir until half of the wine has evaporated. Add dashi if you wish. This will give the dish a more umami flavor.
4. Stir in cordyceps and cook for about a minute. Cordyceps that have been cooked for too long will be rubbery in texture. After a minute, they should be softened.

5. Add strained pasta and spaghetti sauce of choice and stir until everything is incorporated.

Now you know everything about the "zombie mushroom" and even have three delicious recipes you can try. There are truly mushrooms and fungi that can help with so many aspects of our lives, from improving our athletic abilities to fighting cancer and tumors. In the next chapter, we will discuss another mushroom known for its antitumor benefits: the maitake mushroom.

8

MAITAKE MUSHROOM: BENEFIT FROM ITS ANTI-TUMOR PROPERTIES

Being told you have a tumor is a terrifying experience. Many negative thoughts can start rolling through your head, such as if it is cancer and what the medical costs are going to be to get treated. When we think of tumors, our minds might automatically go to what is known as malignant tumors, or those associated with cancer, and can be very harmful to the body. What we don't remember, though, is that there are benign tumors that are relatively harmless but can evolve into something harmful in the future. Additionally, there are many ways to prevent tumors' growth or stop them from developing into something harmful or even cancer. The maitake mushrooms have been shown to have a lot of anti-tumor properties, and eating them allows one to get the necessary nutrients to help the body naturally fight tumors.

Maitake mushrooms, also called the hen of the woods or the dancing mushroom, grow between August and November at the base of hardwood trees such as oak trees. These mushrooms are native to temperate forests and can be used for their medicinal properties and cooking. They are a favorite in Japan and China because of their delicious flavor and the medicinal qualities you can get from them.

HEALTH BENEFITS OF MAITAKE MUSHROOMS

The studies around maitake mushrooms have not been as comprehensive as those done on mushrooms like the turkey tail; however, there have been numerous studies on the mushroom. Many of these studies focus on the cancer-fighting and anti-tumor properties of maitake mushrooms; however, there have been preliminary studies on other benefits such as heart health and helping with type 2 diabetes.

Although no concrete studies have been done to confirm these hypotheses, scientists believe they could help with low or high blood pressure, cold and flu, and reduce inflammation based on what is already known about the maitake mushrooms.

Cancer-fighting and Anti-Tumor Properties

Animal and human studies have found evidence of the maitake mushroom being able to fight cancer and help to reduce the growth of tumors and help prevent them from forming. Studies in mice showed that maitake mushrooms increase the number of tumor-fighting cells and suppress the development of the tumors (Cronkleton, 2016). The studies with mice had them taking maitake orally. This means that the effectiveness of taking extracts from the maitake mushroom and creating medicine from them and given through an IV is not known.

Maitake mushrooms are incredibly effective against cancer and tumors because they attack them by increasing the immune system's effectiveness and the number of cancer-fighting cells. Maitake mushrooms improve the effectiveness of our immune systems by increasing interleukin-1, lymphokines, and interleukin-2. These mushrooms also increase our good friends, the natural killer cells, as we have talked about before, as well as cytotoxic T-cells (Tc), which both attack tumor cells (Mayell, 2001).

Studies of the maitake mushrooms have revealed that it helps battle cancer in three ways:

1. Prevents cancer cells from metastasizing.

2. Slows and stops the growth of tumors.
3. Protects healthy cells from damage that can cause them to become cancerous.

Studies have also considered a fourth possible way for these mushrooms to help with cancer, but the evidence is not as solid as the other three. The fourth possible way maitake mushrooms can help treat cancer is to promote the good effects of chemotherapy and reduce the adverse side effects such as hair loss, nausea, and pain (Mayell, 2001).

Possibly Promotes Better Heart Health

Although there have been no human studies conducted on how maitake mushrooms might improve heart health, animal studies have given preliminary results that it could. Mice were fed freeze-dried maitake mushrooms for four weeks, and cholesterol levels were reduced (Shields, n.d.). Maitake mushrooms also contain the trace mineral copper, which is essential for heart health as it helps maintain healthy heart rates and red blood cell production.

Might Help with Type 2 Diabetes

Studies of rats showed that maitake mushrooms could positively affect blood glucose levels (Cronkleton, 2016). There have been no human studies, but the effects that the maitake mushroom had on the rats is a good sign that these mushrooms might be able to treat and regulate type 2 diabetes.

HOW TO GROW MAITAKE MUSHROOMS

Maitake mushrooms are some of the hardest mushrooms to grow, which is why they are not widely cultivated like the shiitake mushrooms or even lion's mane mushrooms. Typically, these mushrooms grow best in the wild, and when you try to cultivate them at home, they tend not to produce much yield, and it can take years for even mycelium to appear, let alone the fruiting body that we consume. If you want to try and grow your own maitake mushrooms, you will want to mimic the environment they grow in.

Materials and equipment needed to grow maitake mushrooms:

- oak log at least six inches wide and three feet long
- 5/16th drill bit and drill
- pre-inoculated maitake dowels
- hammer or rubber mallet
- beeswax or cheese wax
- paintbrush

Follow these steps to grow your own maitake mushrooms:

1. Soak log for at least six hours in cold water.
2. Drill 1.5 inch deep holes, leaving space in between. One log should have 30 holes.
3. Insert pre-inoculated maitake dowels and seal with melted wax and the paintbrush. Seal any holes that are unused as well.
4. Keep logs outdoors in a damp spot and standing. Water every two weeks to keep moist.
5. After six months, if the dowels start to have signs of growth, then soak the log for 24 hours in ice water to shock the fungi into growing. If

there is no sign of growth, continue to wait. Remember, the mycelium can take a long time to start to form.
6. Keep the logs propped up and wait for your maitake to grow. After your first harvest, it can take up to 6 weeks to see more regrowth.

How to Harvest Maitake Mushrooms

Before you can harvest your maitake mushroom, you need to be able to identify it. Because they grow during the late summer and fall, these mushrooms can be very large, around 20 pounds on average—but they have been recorded as being as heavy as 50 pounds—making them the biggest mushrooms that we have talked about so far. These fungi are characterized as a cluster of smaller mushroom caps that are flat and brown with white edges. The underneath of these mushrooms looks similar to cauliflower or broccoli as their stems for a structure for the caps to overlap. A good rule of thumb to remember: the larger the maitake mushroom, the lighter the color it will have.

Maitake mushrooms, especially fresh maitake mushrooms, are expensive because they only grow a few months out of the year. They can also be very hard to cultivate. The rarity of these mushrooms and their short lifespan are not the only reason they have a high price tag. One pound of maitake mushrooms is sold for about $60. These mushrooms are under a lot of demand, not only by the public, but also by health companies and even chefs. This is why prices tend to rise, as there is only a limited quality available. Harvesting maitake mushrooms is labor-intensive, also causing an increase in pricing.

To harvest your maitake mushrooms, you will want to utilize your sense of smell. Maitake mushrooms that have not reached maturity will have a pleasant smell. Once these mushrooms mature, they will smell terrible. You want to harvest these mushrooms before they reach maturity. Once they do, their texture and taste will change from tender to woody and bitter.

Maitake mushrooms will be found near the bases of trees as they are not particularly fond of sunlight and can be hard to find. The stems of these mushrooms can be very thick, so ripping the mushroom away from the base of the tree isn't a viable option, as it will only damage the mushroom, which can cause issues with preservation later on. Once you have found your maitake mushroom, you will need a knife to cut through the mushroom's stem.

How to Clean Maitake Mushrooms

These mushrooms require a lot of cleaning as they grow at the bases of trees or in clusters. These combined factors lead to a lot of debris and dirt trapped between the mushroom caps. Growing at the base of trees also makes them more susceptible to coming in contact with wild animals and insects.

To start cleaning your maitake mushrooms, you will want to look for any large pieces of debris, such as sticks, leaves, or chunks of soil. Once the larger debris is cleared, take a toothbrush and remove any stubborn dirt and debris. After you have cleaned the mushroom, you will need to cut parts of the stem off. The parts of the mushroom closest to the base will be hard and inedible, and unnecessary to keep when preserving and cooking.

After you have cleared all the debris and cut the hard stems off, look for any signs of mold, insect activity, or bruising. Remove any sections that have these signs. If there is still dirt or debris, use a damp paper towel to wipe it away. Never soak your maitake mushrooms as they will absorb the water, making them more prone to molding, especially if you do not preserve them right away.

How to Store and Preserve Maitake Mushrooms

After the work of finding your mushrooms, harvesting them, and cleaning them, you don't want any to go to waste. You will want to store and preserve any maitake mushrooms you will not use right away so that they do not start to go rancid and are completely unusable.

You can preserve maitake mushrooms using two different methods. The first is to dry them using a food dehydrator or the oven. Make sure to cut these mushrooms into slices or chunks to dry evenly. Drying these mushrooms can cause them to lose some of their nutrition and flavor, unlike the other mushrooms that we have talked about so far in the book, so be sure to keep that in mind when using this method.

The second way to preserve these mushrooms is to freeze them. You can freeze them raw or after you have boiled or sauteed them. To freeze these mushrooms, follow these steps:

1. Cut the mushroom into slices or chunks.
2. Prepare them if you wish, or leave them raw.
3. Lay them on a cookie sheet and freeze.
4. Once they are frozen, transfer them into an airtight freezer bag and write the date they were frozen and six months from them. The freshness of these mushrooms will only last

about six months, so it's best to eat them before the six months have passed.

How to Cook Maitake Mushrooms

Maitake mushrooms are great for cooking, whether you are using your frozen maitake mushrooms or fresh. The taste of these mushrooms is earthy and peppery but can be added to a variety of dishes. Maitake mushrooms should be served cooked and added to stews, soups, sandwiches, omelets. They can be made into their own side dish or an entire meal. If you are cooking with frozen maitake mushrooms, do not thaw them before cooking; throw them right into the pot or pan frozen. The mushrooms can become very soggy and difficult to cook when you thaw them.

If you are cleaning fresh maitake mushrooms, you can pull them apart until they form three-inch slices. You don't need to use a knife, although a knife is recommended if you would rather have a cleaner cut or need to cut the mushroom down the middle. Follow these steps for a quick way to make maitake mushrooms that can be added to soba noodles, pizza, ramen, or stir fry:

1. Pull the mushroom apart to form the slices or cut if desired.

2. Heat a skillet over medium-high heat and add sesame oil.
3. Add maitake mushroom and cook for one minute on each side.
4. Add soy sauce, garlic, and any other seasoning and cook for another minute.

This recipe can be eaten on its own or added to the dishes I described. You can also change this recipe to better suit your tastes while still following the directions.

Before we move on to talking about another medicinal mushroom you can try, here are two more recipes for you to try with maitake mushrooms.

Roasted Maitake Mushrooms and Seaweed Butter

Ingredients:

- 1 1/4 pounds of maitake mushrooms, whole heads recommended
- 1 cup of boiling water
- 1/2 cup of dried seaweed
- 1/4 cup of extra-virgin olive oil
- 1 stick of unsalted butter
- 2 tablespoons of chives, chopped
- salt and pepper to taste
- optional: spices of choice and lemon wedges

Directions:

1. Add seaweed to boiling water until soft and pliable. This will take about 30 minutes.
2. Preheat the oven to 425 degrees Fahrenheit.
3. Strain the seaweed and chop it before adding it to a bowl with butter, salt, and pepper. Stir ingredients until everything is mixed together.
4. Coat the mushroom lightly with olive oil, salt, and pepper, and then place on a baking tray. You can add more seasonings here if you wish.
5. Add 3/4 of the seaweed butter on top of the mushroom, setting the rest to the side.
6. Roast the mushrooms for 30 minutes. Bast the mushrooms occasionally, if it's looking really dry. The mushrooms will be done when they are tender and golden, with a few crispy spots.
7. Serve with chives and the remaining seaweed butter. You can also serve this with a lemon wedge for a splash of citrus.

Creamy One Pan Chicken and Maitake Mushroom

Ingredients:

- 8 ounces of mushrooms of choice
- 3.5 ounces of torn maitake mushrooms
- 2 boneless, skinless chicken breasts

- 4 cloves of sliced garlic
- 2 thinly sliced shallots
- 2 cups of chicken stock
- 1 cup of all-purpose flour
- 1 cup of heavy cream or milk
- 1/2 cup of parmesan cheese, grated
- 2 tablespoons of butter
- 1 tablespoon of olive oil
- 2 sprigs of fresh thyme
- 1 sprig of fresh rosemary
- salt and pepper to taste

Directions:

1. Prepare the mushrooms, shallot, and garlic by slicing them and tearing the maitake mushrooms into small pieces.
2. Pound chicken breasts until they are about 1/2 inch thick. Season with salt and pepper and then dredge with flour.
3. Heat oil and butter in a large cast-iron skillet until the butter has melted and started to bubble. This should take about 3-4 minutes.
4. Add chicken and cook until golden brown, about 5-6 minutes per side. Remove chicken and set to the side.
5. Add mushrooms, shallots, salt, and pepper and

cook for 6-8 minutes over medium heat. The mushrooms should be softened after this. Stir the mixture, so they do not stick.
6. Add garlic, rosemary, and thyme and cook for a minute or until fragrant. Stir them, so they become coated.
7. Add milk, chicken stock, and parmesan, and cook for 4-5 minutes. The mixture should start to thicken, so be sure to stir it to clump up.
8. Add chicken back into the pan. Cook for 8-10 minutes over medium heat. The sauce should be thickened at this point.

Now that you have three new recipes to try with your maitake mushrooms, it's time to talk about a mushroom known worldwide and the most cultivated for its culinary and medicinal uses: the oyster mushroom.

OYSTER MUSHROOMS

Oyster mushrooms are one of the most popular mushrooms eaten, and are widely cultivated for how easy they are to grow and their delicious taste. They are incredibly versatile and can be added to various dishes, including stir fry, toast, pasta, soups, and stews. Oyster mushrooms take after their namesake with their short or absent stem and oyster-shaped cap, and are typically light gray to grayish. Other species can appear pink or yellow in color. While these mushrooms do not taste like oysters, they are still savory with a hint of seafood taste. Oyster mushrooms are not only delicious and widely cultivated, but they are also packed with nutrients and offer so many benefits.

BENEFITS OF OYSTER MUSHROOMS

There are so many benefits that come from eating oyster mushrooms. Although some of the benefits still need more studies, there are very promising results from many of the studies that have been conducted.

Improves Immune Support

The oyster mushroom is full of nutrients, minerals, and compounds that all work to support our immunity. Beta-glucan fiber can be derived from the oyster mushroom and has been shown to have numerous benefits, including antibacterial and antiviral effects. Beta-glucan is a compound that helps regulate the immune system, meaning that it can help to increase activity or reduce it.

Specifically, scientists can derive the beta-glucan fiber pleuran, which is actively used to treat many illnesses. Pleuran has been used to treat recurrent respiratory tract infections in children and upper respiratory tract infections in athletes. After these treatments, children saw a significant decrease in the symptoms (Kubala, 2021).

Further studies showed that those with HSV-1 (herpes simplex virus type-1) had a more significant decrease in symptoms when treated with pleuran, a zinc supplement, and vitamin C, than those that were only treated with vitamin C (Kubala, 2021).

Immune system functioning as a whole also saw improvement when people were taking an oyster mushroom extract. People who took the extract for eight weeks showed an increase in interferon-y, a chemical that helps to protect the body from infection (Kubala, 2021). The increased production of this chemical is a marker of the immune system becoming stronger.

However, the studies that have been conducted on this mushroom's effects have only looked at the benefits that come from the extracts of this mushroom. No studies have researched the impacts of just eating the mushroom on an individual.

Can Improve Heart Health

Oyster mushrooms reduce the risk of heart disease by lowering blood pressure and cholesterol, and improving our overall heart health. Remember, beta-glucan? Well, it is also responsible for the oyster mushrooms' ability to improve our heart health. Short-chain fatty acids, created when our gut bacteria ferment beta-glucan fibers, help to reduce the production of cholesterol, lowering our overall cholesterol levels.

Studies of the oyster mushroom have confirmed that consuming it can help to reduce bad cholesterol, triglycerides, and total cholesterol. One study had 20 people split into two groups. The first group was given soup that contained 30 grams of dried oyster mushrooms. The second group was given soup with no added oyster mushrooms. The contestants then had to eat the soup for 21 days. The contestants who were given the dried oyster mushrooms had decreased cholesterol levels, triglycerides, and bad cholesterol in comparison to the group that was on the placebo (Kubala, 2021).

Many mushroom species have the same nutrients, minerals, and compounds but at varying levels. This is what allows for some mushrooms to have different benefits. The very common white button mushroom contains beta-glucan; but, there is one true winner when you compare it to oyster mushrooms. Oyster mushrooms have about twice as many beta-glucans as white button mushrooms. You might want to consider this the next time you shop for mushrooms at the grocery store.

Can Promote Blood Sugar Regulation

Studies have shown that the oyster mushroom might help regular blood sugar levels, a benefit seen in people with type 2 diabetes and those without. One study of

22 people, some with type 2 diabetes and some without, showed that powdered oyster mushrooms reduced post-meal blood sugar levels (Kubala, 2021).

Oyster mushrooms are effective in reducing both fasting and post-meal blood sugar levels. In 2007, a study of 30 hospitalized type 2 diabetes patients showed that fasting blood sugar was reduced by 22%, and post-meal blood sugar was reduced by 23% after seven days of eating the mushroom. The effects of the mushroom also did not dissipate immediately after they were digested. After a week of not eating oyster mushrooms, the patients still saw effects as fasting blood sugar was reduced by 13% and post-meal blood sugar by 20% (Kubala, 2021).

The oyster mushroom's ability to reduce blood sugar levels is attributed to two things. The first is that it inhibits proteins known for increasing blood sugar from being produced. The second is that it promotes an increase of sugar usage in the body's tissues, causing a reduction in blood sugar levels. Once again, the compound beta-glucan is attributed to these abilities as its a fiber that slows down the digestion and absorption of carbohydrates, thus reducing blood sugar levels from spiking.

Other Possible Benefits

These possible benefits have had no solid evidence behind them to show if humans would see the same effects, but test-tube and animals studies have shown that the oyster mushroom is possibly capable of giving us the following benefits:

1. It might have anti-inflammatory effects: rats that had inflammation in their paws saw a significant reduction after consuming oyster mushrooms.
2. It might have anti-tumor effects: animal and test-tube studies have revealed that it might have possible anti-tumor effects; however, more studies need to be conducted to conclude this.
3. It might improve gut health: rodent studies revealed that eating oyster mushrooms decreased unhealthy bacteria and increased compounds such as short-chain fatty acids in our guts.

There are no known risks from consuming the oyster mushroom. The rate of their cultivation and how commonly they are ingested shows this. However, if you are sensitive to other mushrooms, avoid consuming these mushrooms.

Now that you know all the benefits of eating oyster mushrooms, you can consider adding them to your diet. There are two ways to add them to your diet: you can either buy them from the store or grow them at home. Growing these mushrooms is extremely easy, and you will learn this in the next section.

HOW TO GROW OYSTER MUSHROOMS

Oyster mushrooms grow worldwide, but their short fruiting life makes it impossible to harvest them all year round. The increased demand for oyster mushrooms had people start cultivating them to access them whenever they needed them. The Germans first cultivated these mushrooms in World War II and have increased nearly 18-fold since the beginning of the German's cultivation. In 1965, 350,000 metric tons of oyster mushrooms were cultivated, and in 1997, 6,160,800 metric tons were cultivated (GroCycle, 2018). That's a lot of oyster mushrooms, and that was over 20 years ago—so you can only imagine how many are grown and harvested now!

Oyster mushrooms were the subject of such a significant boom in cultivation because they are very easy to grow, grow quickly, and have various health benefits, which we have talked about. Oyster mushrooms are available almost everywhere, but growing them is always fulfilling, so here is a step-by-step for you to follow to grow your own.

Materials and equipment needed to grow oyster mushrooms:

- oyster mushroom spawn
- the substrate material of choice
- growing containers or bags

Follow these steps to grow your own oyster mushrooms.

Step 1: Prepare to grow your mushrooms. As with any project, you need to prepare your own mushrooms at home:

1. The first thing you need to do is pick the species of oyster mushrooms you want to grow. Later in the chapter, there will be a list of the common species of oyster mushrooms that you might find while foraging in the wild. You will want to pick an oyster mushroom that will grow in the climate you live in. The pearl oyster is the most common and is very easy to grow.
2. After picking your oyster mushroom species, you must choose a substrate in which you will grow your mushrooms. The great thing about oyster mushrooms is that they are not super picky about the substrate they grow in and will do just fine in a variety of them. Common substrates used with oyster mushrooms include straw, sawdust, wood pellets, coffee grounds, and cardboard.
3. Now that you have decided on the species and substrate you will use, it's time to order the supplies. You will need to buy the oyster mushrooms spawn of choice, your substrate, and plastic bags or containers if you do not already have them.

Step 2: Prepare the substrate. The substrate is what is going to give your mushrooms nutrients and food to develop. Without it, the mushroom's mycelium is not going to form. There are various ways to prepare your substrate that will differ depending on the kind of substrate you are using:

1. Sawdust pellets: soak equal weight water and pellets for 30 minutes. Break up the pellets by mixing them.
2. Cardboard and straw: soak straw in hot water for 1-2 hours or cold water for 12-18 hours. If you are using hot water, it should be around 149-176 degrees Fahrenheit. The cold water also needs to be a high-pH lime bath.
3. Coffee grounds: use grounds that were at most brewed 24 hours ago. If your coffee grounds are more than 24 hours old, they are more prone to molding, which will hinder your oyster mushrooms from growing. There is no preparation needed other than to mix the coffee grounds with at least 20-50% straw.

Step 3: Add your mushroom spawn to your substrate. This process is also called inoculation.

1. Make sure that your workspace and hands are clean before this process. This will stop unwanted germs and viruses from entering your mushrooms' new home.

2. Check the moisture of your substrate. There needs to be moisture in the substrate but not too much that it causes everything to mold. To check the moisture level, squeeze a handful tightly. If water comes out, it still needs time to dry; however, it's too dry if it doesn't hold its shape.
3. In a plastic bin, mix your mushroom spawn with your substrate. Transfer this into your growing vessel; for the sake of these instructions, we will use plastic bags.
4. Tie the top of the bag with a rubber band or paperclip.

Step 4: Incubate your mushrooms. This is a vital stage. Your mushroom spawns are going to start growing mycelium.

1. Incubate your oyster mushrooms between 20-24 degrees Celsius. You should store them somewhere dark.
2. You do not need to do anything except wait for the mycelium to start to form. Your mushrooms will be ready for the next step when the bag is fully white.
3. When your mushrooms are incubating, be sure to watch for any signs of blue or green starting

to grow. This is a sign that mold is growing, and the bag will need to be thrown away.

Step 5: Fruiting your mushrooms. This is the step that all your preparation and waiting was preparing for. Mushrooms start to grow when there are changes to the environment or run out of food.

1. Once the bag has become colonized, shown when it is white, it's time to change the environment to allow the fruiting bodies to grow.
2. Poke holes or cut a square into the bag to signal room to grow to the mycelium.
3. Move the bags into an area with indirect light and spray the bags twice a day to keep the humidity levels up.
4. In as little as seven days, you will see mushrooms starting to form, and 5-7 days after that, they will nearly double in size.
5. After the edges of the caps start to flatten, it's time to harvest. However, this doesn't mean the end of your growing journey. Continue to water the cut endings, and 1-2 weeks later, your oyster mushrooms will start to grow.

After your mushrooms have started to grow, it's time to harvest them. But what if you are going out to forage in nature? How will you identify what mushrooms are oyster mushrooms? Keep reading to learn how to identify oyster mushrooms and harvest them.

How to Identify and Harvest Oyster Mushrooms

Oyster mushrooms are readily available in many stores as there is a huge market for cultivating and producing oyster mushrooms. However, sometimes there is nothing more fulfilling than going out and trying to forage for oyster mushrooms. There are nearly 40 species of oyster mushrooms that can be found worldwide. These mushrooms form on trees and logs that have fallen and typically will grow after the first frost of the year in the fall. Oyster mushrooms will grow on the underside of the logs as they don't like the sun and will typically grow in clusters. Oak and beech trees are the most common places these mushrooms will grow.

As aforementioned, these mushrooms grow fast, so you will want to harvest soon after the first frost. You want to harvest these mushrooms when they are young because they become leathery and inedible as they mature. There are various species of oyster mushrooms that you might encounter in the wild. All of these species are edible, with slight changes in their taste and appearance; however, the benefits of these mushrooms are relatively the same. The most common types of oyster mushrooms you will encounter include:

- **Pearl oyster:** the most common species and found throughout North America. These mushrooms have a woodsy and slightly sweet taste.
- **Golden oyster:** named after its bright yellow color and has a more aromatic and complex taste.
- **Pink oyster:** pink in appearance and has ruffled caps. The pink color fades when cooked, and these mushrooms tend to be tough and woody.
- **Blue oyster:** are not bright blue, but rather are gray in with a blue tinge. These mushrooms have bright gills and dark caps and taste like pearl oyster mushrooms.
- **Phoenix oyster:** the caps of this species are smaller and paler and will have a longer stem than other mushrooms. This species will grow in the late summer as they prefer warmer weather.
- **King oyster:** a species that looks nothing like the other oyster mushroom species. This species has thin brown-colored caps and thick white stems.

Oyster mushrooms have various defining features that you can look for when harvesting. The most recognizable part of the oyster mushroom is the cap. These mushrooms should have smooth caps that form in overlapping clusters. The caps are shaped like oysters or fans and vary between 5-25 centimeters. The gills of oyster mushrooms run down most of the stem if there is one. If there are stems, they are typically very stubby and will grow off-centered. Oyster mushrooms grow on dead trees and logs, so avoid any if they are growing on a living tree.

Lookalike mushroom species to avoid include:

- **Elm oyster:** it is not an actual oyster mushroom but looks very similar. However, the gills of this species do not run down the entire stem, which is the marker that it isn't an oyster mushroom.
- **Ghost fungus:** known to grow in Australia and Japan. These mushrooms glow in the dark, which is not a characteristic of oyster mushrooms.
- **Jack-O-Lantern mushroom:** has bioluminescent properties and is found in Europe, Mexico, California, and some parts of North America. They are bright orange and

easy to avoid. These mushrooms can cause nausea, diarrhea, and cramping.

- **Ivory funnel:** tend to grow in meadows, which is the first step to knowing it isn't an oyster mushroom. These inedible mushrooms will cause side effects such as stomach pain, diarrhea, nausea, and trouble breathing.

Harvesting your oyster mushrooms is a very easy process. After you have identified that the mushroom you are picking is an oyster mushroom, make sure that the mushroom isn't too old. An oyster mushroom is too old if the edges are starting to darken at the edges, or if the mushroom feels dry or is starting to harden. You can use your hands for smaller mushrooms and scissors for larger ones. To use your hands, just pinch the base and twist, and the mushroom will rip away. Use scissors to snip the mushrooms away from the base for larger mushrooms.

How to Clean and Store Oyster Mushrooms

Do not clean your oyster mushrooms until you are going to use them. Cleaning them can make them go bad faster in the fridge. If you are buying or harvesting fresh oyster mushrooms, take them out of any packaging and place them in a paper bag, wrapping them loosely. Wrapping them too tightly will not allow moisture to escape and cause the mushrooms to go bad. Store your mushrooms in the central part of your fridge for up to a week. Never use plastic for storing your mushrooms as the moisture will not be absorbed, causing your mushrooms to go soggy.

Oyster mushrooms are porous; thus, they act like a sponge when interacting with water. You want to clean your oyster mushrooms with as little water as possible. However, there might be some instances where you need to use a little water. When cleaning your oyster mushrooms, there are three methods you can use. The first method is to wipe the mushrooms off with a damp paper towel. This allows you to get any dirt and debris off. Make sure the paper towel is only slightly damp and light on the pressure as you don't want to damage the oyster mushrooms. The second method you can use is a toothbrush or mushroom brush to wipe any debris off the mushrooms. You can also slightly dampen the brush for more challenging spots. The third method is to rinse the mushrooms underwater using a colander quickly. Do not let the mushrooms sit in water and quickly dry them off if you use this method.

After you have cleaned your mushrooms, you can prepare them one of two ways. You can dry them or freeze them. For beginners, freezing is recommended because it is easier to use later. To freeze your mushroom, follow these steps:

1. Remove the stem with a knife; typically, the stem is hard and inedible.
2. Sautee your mushrooms in olive oil or butter until liquids are released from the mushroom.
3. Remove from pan and allow to cool before transferring them to a freezer bag and putting them in the freezer. Keep up to six months in the freezer.
4. To use them, do not thaw as they will become soggy. Rather, just toss the mushrooms into the pan when you are ready to use them, and they heat up quickly.

The second method of preserving and storing oyster mushrooms is to dry them. Cut the stem off and cut into slices before drying your mushrooms out. You can use your oven at the lowest setting or a food dehydrator. You can then leave these mushrooms as they are or use a mortar and pestle to turn them into a powder. Store your dried mushrooms in air-tight containers and out of direct sunlight. You can use oyster mushroom powder in various dishes, including adding to smoothies, stews, and soups, or even add to batter in desserts for a boost of nutrients.

How to Cook Oyster Mushrooms Plus Five Recipes

Oyster mushrooms are one of the most versatile mushrooms with their very mild seafood taste. It is also one of the easiest mushrooms to cook. There are numerous ways to consume oyster mushrooms, but their availability all year round and ease of use make them the most commonly eaten fresh. After you have harvested your mushrooms, there are various ways you can cook your oyster mushrooms. Here are five recipes for you to try with your oyster mushrooms.

Mushroom Stir Fry

Ingredients:

- 300 grams of your vegetables of choice
- 200 grams of oyster mushrooms
- 150 grams of egg noodles
- 4 tablespoons of water
- 4 tablespoons of soy sauce
- 3 tablespoons of toasted sesame oil
- 1 teaspoon of fresh ginger, grated
- 1 or 2 cloves of minced garlic
- slice of lemon
- optional: sesame seeds and bean sprouts

Directions:

1. Cook the egg noodles by following the directions on the packet, and prep vegetables and mushrooms by slicing them into a desirable size. After the egg noodles are done, drain them and place them in a bowl of cold water.
2. Heat a frying pan over high heat and add sesame oil once it starts to smoke. Once the sesame oil is heated, add ginger and garlic. Stir for 30 seconds and add mushrooms.
3. Cook mushrooms for 3-4 minutes or until the mushrooms start to brown. Add the vegetables and cook for another 4-5 minutes.
4. Add soy water, soy sauce, egg noodles, and sesame seeds and bean sprouts if you use them.
5. Stir until the liquid evaporates and take off heat one minute later.
6. Squeeze lemon juice in, give one final stir, and enjoy.

Mushrooms on Toast

Ingredients:

- 2 slices of bread of choice
- 200 grams of oyster mushrooms
- olive oil or butter of choice

- salt and pepper to taste
- optional: any additional topping you want

Directions:

1. Prep mushrooms, either by slicing them or pulling them apart.
2. Heat a pan and add olive oil or butter. Add mushrooms and season with salt and pepper. Cook for 5-10 minutes, stirring frequently.
3. Toast bread and top with any desirable toppings before scooping mushrooms out of the pan and serving on top of toast.

Thai Mushroom Soup

Ingredients:

- 200 grams of oyster mushrooms
- 200 grams of spinach
- 2 cups of vegetable stock of water
- 1 cup of coconut milk
- 3 tablespoons of light soy sauce
- 3 tablespoons of lime juice
- 2-3 chilis, cut and smashed
- 3 kaffir lime leaves
- 2 lemongrass stalks, cut into five centimeters pieces, and smashed

- fresh or dried coriander

Directions:

1. Prepare mushrooms by cutting them into small chunks.
2. Bring vegetable stock to a boil and add lime leaves and lemongrass.
3. Simmer vegetable stock for 5 minutes, and then add coconut milk, chilis, mushrooms, and spinach.
4. Simmer for another 5 minutes. The mushrooms should be soft at this point. If not, increase the heat and simmer for a few more minutes.
5. Remove from heat and stir in soy sauce, lime juice, or coriander.
6. Serve hot and enjoy.

Cream of Mushroom Soup

Ingredients:

- 200 grams of oyster mushrooms
- 100 grams of chestnut mushrooms
- 10 grams of dried wild mushroom
- 750 milliliters of chicken or vegetable stock
- 200 milliliters of double cream or creme fraiche
- 100 milliliters of white wine

- 3 tablespoons of olive oil
- 1 tablespoon of butter
- 3 diced shallots
- 2 sliced garlic cloves
- chopped parsley and chives

Directions:

1. Soak dried mushrooms for 15 minutes in 250 milliliters of hot water.
2. Drain and add water to chicken or vegetable stocks.
3. Heat butter and 2 tablespoons of olive oil in a saucepan over medium-high heat. Fry mushrooms until they are brown on the edges. Depending on the size of your saucepan, you might need to do this in batches. Set the mushrooms to the side.
4. Add the remaining tablespoon of oil and reduce heat to low. Fry shallots for 6-7 minutes or until soft, then add garlic. Cook for two minutes.
5. Add white wine and boil for two minutes until it becomes a glaze. Add stock and boil for 3-4 minutes.
6. Add mushrooms to the stock and simmer for 5 minutes.

7. Use a blender to puree your soup, and then put it back into the pan. Add the cream and simmer for another 5 minutes before adding seasoning, parsley, or chives.

Oyster Mushroom Stroganoff

Ingredients:

- 300 milliliters of vegetable stock
- 100 milliliters of white wine
- 200 grams of oyster mushrooms
- 100 grams of chestnut mushrooms
- 4 tablespoons of creme fraiche
- 2 tablespoons of olive oil
- 1 tablespoon of butter
- 1 tablespoon of flour
- 1 tablespoon of paprika
- 1 onion
- 2 garlic cloves
- juice from half a lemon

Directions:

1. Fry garlic and onion with oil and butter for 7 minutes. The onions should be soft and translucent.
2. Chop mushrooms into small chunks and

increase heat to medium-high. Add mushrooms and cook for 5 minutes. Stir in paprika and flour until they coat the mushrooms.
3. Add wine and stir. Boil for a minute or two, and then add the stock. Boil for five minutes or until the mixture thickens.
4. Add creme fraiche, mix well, and ensure it heats through. Add seasoning and lemon juice.

Oyster mushrooms are one of the most common mushrooms you can buy or grow, and they come with some fantastic benefits. Their versatile nature makes it so easy to include in any meal and reap the health benefits you want. We have one more mushroom to talk about, and this mushroom comes with a variety of benefits. And that mushroom is the wood ear mushroom, also known as black fungus.

WOOD EAR MUSHROOM

The wood ear mushroom, also known as black fungus or cloud ear fungus, is a mushroom species that grows in China and tropical areas, including Nigeria, Hawaii, India, and the Pacific Islands. These mushrooms grow on the fallen logs and tree trunks, and they are commercially cultivated. However, they are not easily grown and do much better while in their native habitats. Growing these mushrooms in North America or Europe doesn't usually work unless someone can set up the right environment. Obtaining the spawn for these mushrooms can also be difficult, making it harder for individuals to grow their own wood ear mushrooms.

POTENTIAL BENEFITS

Although these mushrooms are extremely popular in China, they are more desired for their culinary uses as they are very versatile. These mushrooms being more desired for their culinary purposes has put them on the back burner for their medicinal uses; however, scientists have started to turn towards wood ear mushrooms to see the different medicinal benefits one can get from this mushroom. As studies are entering the beginning stages, these are all potential benefits that still need a little more research behind them to guarantee these mushrooms will give you these benefits.

Help Immune and Gut Health

Remember that the gut and the immune system are tightly linked. Our gut health directly impacts our immune health and vice versa. Eating prebiotics helps to improve digestive health and maintain regular bowel movements. Wood ear mushrooms boost prebiotics, which feeds our healthy gut bacteria. The improvement in gut health from wood ear mushrooms then helps promote immune health, which can then help treat numerous other issues in the body. This is the most researched and agreed on benefit from the wood ear mushroom of all the benefits.

Improve Brain Health

The lion's mane mushrooms, as we know, are one of the mushrooms that can help with improving brain health. Wood ear mushrooms have also been shown to improve brain health possibly. One test-tube study has shown that wood ear mushrooms can inhibit beta-secretase activity, an enzyme responsible for releasing beta-amyloid proteins linked to Alzheimer's and dementia (Wartenberg, 2019). More studies on humans need to be done to see just how powerful this effect would be on humans or if we would see any from consuming the wood ear mushroom.

Lower Cholesterol

The wood ear mushrooms contain polyphenols that help to lower bad cholesterol. Lowering bad cholesterol helps to reduce heart disease and improve heart health. Studies on rabbits showed that those who ate wood ear mushrooms saw a decrease in bad and total cholesterol (Wartenberg, 2019). No studies have been conducted on humans to see if they would get the same effects.

May Protect the Liver

Some medicinal mushrooms can be hard on the liver, and many toxic mushrooms target the liver and kidneys. We often don't think about the importance of these organs; however, they are essential for our health and need to be protected. Studies on rats showed that a mixture of powdered wood ear mushrooms and water effectively reversed the symptoms and protected the liver from an overdose of acetaminophen, commonly known as Tylenol (Wartenberg, 2019). More studies need to be conducted on other drugs to see which ones the wood ear mushroom could protect against and if the same effects would occur in humans.

Risks Associated with Wood Ear Mushrooms and Where to Get Them

There are no risks associated with eating the wood ear mushrooms that have been dried and bought from commercial suppliers. Mushrooms that have been commercially dried and sold will be the safest as they have been properly identified as wood ear mushrooms. These mushrooms are dried and then sold as they do not keep fresh for long.

It is not recommended for individuals to go out and harvest the wood ear mushroom and eat raw. These mushrooms have many lookalikes that can be poisonous and can even be fatal when consumed. These fungi also absorb the pollutants in the environment, leading to unhealthy bacteria growing and adverse reactions when eaten.

Cooking these mushrooms or rehydrating dried wood ear mushrooms and then cooking kills off any harmful bacteria that might have grown on them. It has also been shown that boiling the mushrooms might increase antioxidant activities, allowing for more benefits.

In China and other Asian countries, dried wood ear mushrooms are readily available. If you do not live in these countries, you will need to go to Asian markets or grocery stores to see if they have any or order them online. Make sure that you are buying from reputable sources when online.

HOW TO REHYDRATE WOOD EAR MUSHROOMS AND RECIPES TO TRY

Dried wood ear mushrooms are the only way someone in non-Asian countries will be able to consume these mushrooms because they are not widely cultivated or grown outside of their natural habitat. Wood ear mushrooms will grow back to the size they were before they were dehydrated, so be mindful of how many you need and how big they are going to get before you rehydrate them.

To rehydrate your wood ear mushrooms, follow these steps:

1. Place mushrooms into a bowl with cold water. Make sure the bowl is large as the mushrooms will expand a lot.
2. Allow the mushrooms to sit in the water for at least two hours. You can also leave them to soak overnight, just place the bowl into the fridge to stay cool.
3. After the mushrooms have become plump, brown, slightly transparent, and springy, wash them by rubbing them with your fingers to remove dirt and debris.
4. Stems are likely to be stiff, so use a knife or scissors to remove them.

If you forgot to rehydrate your mushrooms and need them for your dinner, you can speed the process up by soaking them in hot water for 20 minutes. However, be aware that rehydrating them like this will impact the texture of your mushrooms.

Now that you know how to rehydrate your wood ear mushrooms, it's time to cook them and get all the health benefits you can from them. Here are four recipes for you to try with your wood ear mushrooms.

Wood Ear Mushroom Salad

This recipe does not cook the wood ear mushrooms, so you will want to use the boiling water method for rehydrating the mushrooms. This ensures that any harmful bacteria are killed.

Ingredients:

- 15 grams of wood ear mushrooms (before rehydrating)
- 1/2 shredded spring onion
- 1/2 julienned small carrot
- 1 minced garlic clove
- 1 teaspoon of light soy sauce
- 1/2 teaspoon of rice vinegar
- 1/2 teaspoon of minced ginger
- 1/4 teaspoon of salt

- roasted sesame seeds for garnish
- optional: chili oil

Directions:

1. Rehydrate your wood ear mushrooms by placing them in boiling water for 20 minutes. Remove any stems or hard pieces.
2. Wash under cold water and shake in a colander or sieve to remove any excess water. Pat dry if they are still really wet.
3. Combine all ingredients into a large bowl and stir to incorporate everything.
4. Place in the fridge and allow to cool for 20-30 minutes before serving.

Wood Ear Mushrooms and Pork Dumplings in Asian Broth

Ingredients:

- 800 milliliters of chicken stock
- 10 grams of wood ear mushrooms (before rehydrating)
- 4 spring onions, white and green parts, separated
- 1 red chili, thinly sliced
- 1 tablespoon of light soy sauce

- 2 teaspoons of black vinegar
- salt and white pepper to taste

Dumplings:

- 10 gow gee wrappers
- 100 grams of minced pork
- 1 tablespoon of green parts of spring onions, finely chopped
- 2 teaspoons of grated ginger
- 1 teaspoon of black vinegar
- 1 teaspoon of soy sauce
- 1 teaspoon of sesame oil

Directions:

1. Rehydrate the mushrooms using the cold water method.
2. Finely chop the wood ear mushrooms, leaving 1 tablespoon to the side.
3. Combine the rest of the mushrooms with chicken stock, chili, white parts of the spring onion, ginger, vinegar, and soy sauce into a pot.
4. Bring to a boil and simmer for 15 minutes. Season with salt and white pepper.
5. Combine all the ingredients and the 1

tablespoon of mushrooms you had set aside. Season with salt and white pepper if needed.
6. Spoon 2 tablespoons of mixture into wrappers. Moisten an edge with water and then fold in half.
7. Use baking paper to line your steamer and steam the dumplings for five minutes.
8. Strain the broth and place it into bowls. Divide the dumplings evenly and put them into the broth. Slice green parts of the spring onion and garnish with it.

Pork Belly with Wood Ear Mushrooms and Peppers

Ingredients:

- 1 cup of wood ear mushroom (before rehydration)
- 1 pound of lean pork belly
- 1 bell pepper
- 1/4 cup of water
- 3 1/2 tablespoons of soy sauce

Direction:

1. Rehydrate the wood ear mushrooms using the cold water method. Prepare the lean pork belly

by slicing it into one-inch slices. Dice bell pepper.
2. Sear pork belly over medium-high heat. Sear all sides until golden brown.
3. Add bell pepper and cook for a few minutes, stirring and tossing them once in a while.
4. Add mushrooms and soy sauce and cook for five minutes.
5. Add water and cover. Reduce heat to medium and simmer for 5-10 minutes.
6. Stir everything together and then serve.

Wood Ear Mushrooms and Bamboo Shoots with Smoky Coconut Rice

Ingredients:

- 1 1/2 cup of water
- 1 cup of basmati rice
- 1 cup of wood ear mushrooms (before rehydration)
- 1/2 cup of coconut milk
- 1/3 cup of bamboo shoots
- 1/3 cup of chopped scallions
- 1 red bell pepper, thinly sliced
- 1-2 tablespoons of sweet chili sauce
- 1 teaspoon of smoked paprika
- salt to taste

Directions:

1. Add rice and water to a pot or wok. Bring to a boil, cover, and cook for five minutes.
2. Add the remaining ingredients, stirring to mix everything.
3. Cook until all liquid is absorbed and rice is cooked; this should take about ten minutes.
4. Serve and enjoy.

We've reached the end of the medicinal mushrooms. We've talked about so many medicinal mushrooms and fungi you can go out and buy, forage, or grow and get a large number of benefits. The nine mushrooms that we have talked about are only the tip of the iceberg. There are so many other mushrooms out there to explore, but the nine mushrooms and fungi species we have talked about are the most common and some of the most researched. Before our journey together ends, let's recap what we have learned.

CONCLUSION

Western ideologies often make us think that healing using natural and holistic methods is not as good as the medicines doctors will prescribe. However, this is false. Mushrooms and fungi are some of nature's most powerful medicines. Taking holistic approaches alongside professional treatment can be the best option for many people dealing with health issues. After the initial health issue has been relieved, you can transition into mostly holistic approaches.

You will decide on your health concerns to choose a specific mushroom. You don't want to choose the wrong mushrooms to grow, forage, or buy because although they might give you health benefits, they might not be the ones that you want. Let's recap the benefits you can get from each mushroom:

1. **Reishi mushrooms** will help boost the immune system, fight depression and fatigue, and fight cancer. The reishi mushroom's ability to help battle fatigue and depression specifically has been shown to help improve sleep. Other benefits that still need more studies conducted include decreased blood sugar levels, heart health improvement, and antioxidant boosts.
2. **Lion's mane mushrooms** are one of the best mushrooms for brain health. These mushrooms help relieve depression and anxiety symptoms, protect against neurodegenerative diseases, and speed up recovery time for nervous system injuries. There are also a few physical benefits.
3. **The Chaga mushroom** is a species that is currently under scientists' eyes as test-tube and animal studies are being conducted. However, scientists are pretty optimistic about the benefits humans can see from Chaga mushrooms, including combating oxidative stress, preventing the formation and growth of cancer, and lowering cholesterol.
4. **Shiitake mushrooms** are renowned for their heart health benefits and other benefits, including strengthening bones and having antibacterial and antiviral properties. These

mushrooms are usually readily available in grocery stores.
5. **The turkey tail mushroom** is one of the most used mushrooms for battling cancer and has numerous immune-boosting benefits, including improving cancer patient immune functions, improving gut health, enhancing the speed and effectiveness of cancer treatments, and is packed full of antioxidants and polysaccharopeptides.
6. **Cordyceps** is a natural energy booster, otherwise known as the zombie caterpillar mushroom. Benefits from consuming cordyceps include athletic performance boosts, anti-aging properties, managing type 2 diabetes, and potentially fighting tumors.
7. **Maitake mushrooms** are another anti-tumor mushroom that has started to make traction in the science world. Benefits of the maitake mushroom include cancer-fighting and anti-tumor benefits and possibly helping to manage type 2 diabetes and promote better heart health. More studies need to be conducted to confirm if the maitake mushroom can help with heart health and type 2 diabetes.
8. **Oyster mushrooms** are one of the most cultivated mushrooms and can be found in

nature worldwide. There are numerous species, many of which will have similar effects, just different appearances. The benefits you can get from oyster mushrooms include improving immune support and heart health, and promoting blood sugar regulation. Potential benefits that need more studies include improved gut health, anti-tumor effects, and anti-inflammatory effects.

9. **Wood ear mushrooms** are only recently undergoing scientific studies, they have a few potential benefits, including improving immune and gut health, improving brain health, lowering cholesterol, and protecting the liver. The wood ear mushroom is mainly used for cooking; however, the benefits you might be able to get from them are promising.

It's important to remember that you need to take a holistic approach when trying to improve your overall health. Yes, going to the doctors and seeking help for an issue is likely to help, but it will only give you a temporary fix. Taking a holistic approach will improve your overall health and allow you to take preventative measures that will drastically decrease your risk of health issues, including heart disease and cancer.

Consuming more medicinal mushrooms is only part of the journey you will take to improve your overall health. Alongside eating healthier, you need to make sure you are exercising, getting enough sleep, and taking care of your mental health. Remember that mental and physical health are tightly linked. You can make all the changes you want to make yourself healthier physically, but if your mental health is not addressed, your physical health will never be at 100%, as your poor mental health will keep dragging it back and vice versa. If you don't change your physical health, your mental health will also improve. You need to work on both simultaneously to ensure your journey is not for nothing.

Overall, starting to eat more medicinal mushrooms is a great first step to your health journey. Growing your own mushrooms or going out and foraging for them has a whole other set of benefits as it allows you to spend time outdoors. Gardening and walking in nature are excellent for both mental and physical health. They help destress, get your body moving, and expose you to vitamins and nutrients you wouldn't get when staying inside.

Growing your own mushrooms or foraging for them can help you save thousands of dollars. Although you might need to pay some upfront costs, you will not need to go to the grocery store to grow mushrooms, and you will be able to store them for a long time, giving you access to medicinal mushrooms even during the offseason. Foraging mushrooms doesn't cost anything other than travel fare, and you can forage more than you are going to use immediately and then preserve them for later use.

Only a few mushrooms that we have talked about can be stored fresh for at most a couple of weeks. You will either need to freeze them or dry them. To freeze your mushrooms, boil or saute them, and then store them in the freezer. When you are ready to use them, toss them directly into the pan. Use a food dehydrator or the oven on the lowest setting to dry them. You can leave the mushrooms as chunks or slices or crush them into a powder. Make sure you store your dried mushroom in air-tight containers and out of direct light. Dried mushrooms can be used in various ways, including teas, capsules, and nutrient boosters to add to stew, soups, and smoothies.

Throughout this book, I have shown you various recipes you can try. Do not be afraid to swap out the types of mushrooms and to try something new. Experimenting with medicinal mushrooms and the different dishes you can make with them is one of the best parts of trying medicinal mushrooms. Don't be afraid to change up the recipes to best suit your needs.

Trying medicinal mushrooms will give your health the boost that you need and give you hope for a healthier future. You have all the tools and information you need to start your medicinal mushroom journey, now use them to improve your health. Hearing about the journeys of others can be incredibly inspiring. Please leave a review and let others know how much medicinal mushrooms have helped you and why others should consider incorporating them into their diets.

A SPECIAL GIFT TO OUR READERS

Herewith your purchase of this book we have included a gift to help you get prepared for the future. Herbal Medicine 101 will not only let you discover more about herbal remedies but let you get involved in the community. This is the key to opening the door for starting your journey.

Scan the QR code below and let us know what email is best to deliver it to.

REFERENCES

Aijaz, B. (2021, April 16). *Some fun facts about mushrooms we bet you didn't know*. IndiaTimes. https://www.indiatimes.com/trending/environment/fun-facts-about-mushrooms-538399.html

Brenner, L. (2018). *How to identify poisonous mushrooms*. Sciencing. https://sciencing.com/identify-poisonous-mushrooms-2057768.html

Brown, M. J. (2018, October 25). *Chaga mushroom: Uses, benefits and side effects*. Healthline. https://www.healthline.com/nutrition/chaga-mushroom#side-effects

Chaga Health. (n.d.). *Chaga farming*. Chaga Health. Retrieved February 3, 2022, from https://chagahealth.eu/en/chaga-farming/

Chun, K. (2014). *Roasted maitake mushrooms with seaweed butter recipe*. Food & Wine. https://www.foodandwine.com/recipes/roasted-maitake-mushrooms-seaweed-butter

Cohut, M. (2019, March 15). *Does eating mushrooms protect brain health?* Medical News Today. https://www.medicalnewstoday.com/articles/324710

Conrad, K. (2020, June 24). *8 most poisonous types of mushrooms*. WorldAtlas. https://www.worldatlas.com/articles/8-most-poisonous-types-of-mushrooms.html

CRCLR. (n.d.). *6 ways mushrooms can help save the planet*. Crclr.org. https://crclr.org/article/2017-05-01-6-ways-mushrooms-can-help-save-the-planet

Cronkleton, E. (2016, October 31). *Everything you should know about maitake mushroom*. Healthline. https://www.healthline.com/health/food-nutrition/maitake-mushroom

Dix, M. (2017, December 13). *Everything you should know about oxidative stress*. Healthline. https://www.healthline.com/health/oxidative-stress

Farnell, S. (2021, September 29). *Creamy one pan maitake mushroom chicken*. Jawns I Cooked. https://jawnsicooked.com/dinner/creamy-one-pan-maitake-mushroom-chicken/#wprm-recipe-container-12599

REFERENCES | 195

Fearon, R. (2020). *Medicinal mushrooms can cure disease*. Discovery. https://www.discovery.com/science/medicinal-mushrooms-are-a-rich-source-of-compounds-to-cure-disea

FreshCap. (2017, July 15). *Growing shiitake mushrooms*. FreshCap Mushrooms. https://learn.freshcap.com/growing/growing-shiitake-mushrooms/

Fulmer, M. (2016, August 5). *Five trending superfoods you need to know about*. Los Angeles Times. https://www.latimes.com/health/la-he-the-new-superfoods-20160711-snap-story.html

Fungi Ally. (n.d.). *Cordyceps cultivation methods: A step-by-step process for growers*. Fungi Ally. Retrieved February 8, 2022, from https://www.fungially.com/blogs/growing-mushrooms/cordyceps-cultivation-methods

Goldman, R. (2017). *Are mushrooms good for you?* Healthline. https://www.healthline.com/health/food-nutrition/are-mushrooms-good-for-you

GroCycle. (2018, September 7). *How to grow oyster mushrooms: the ultimate step by step guide*. GroCycle. https://grocycle.com/how-to-grow-oyster-mushrooms/

Grow Wild. (n.d.). *Harvesting your oyster mushroom*. GrowWildUK. Retrieved February 11, 2022, from

REFERENCES

https://www.growwilduk.com/harvesting-your-oyster-mushroom

Guo, W. (2021, March 20). *Wood ear mushroom, how to rehydrate and cook (木 耳)*. Red House Spice. https://redhousespice.com/wood-ear-mushroom-salad/

Harvard T.H. Chan School of Public Health. (2020, March 19). *Mushrooms*. The Nutrition Source. https://www.hsph.harvard.edu/nutritionsource/food-features/mushrooms/

itsfoodtastic. (n.d.). *Ultimate guide on how to store shiitake mushrooms*. ItsFoodtastic. Retrieved February 4, 2022, from https://itsfoodtastic.com/ultimate-guide-on-how-to-store-shiitake-mushrooms/

Jefferson, R. S. (2019). *Researchers now say mushrooms may reduce risk of cognitive decline*. Forbes. https://www.forbes.com/sites/robinseatonjefferson/2019/03/21/maybe-theyre-all-magic-researchers-now-say-mushrooms-may-reduce-risk-of-cognitive-decline/?sh=1399e93c2160

Jennings, K.-A. (2019, June 14). *Why shiitake mushrooms are good for you*. Healthline. https://www.healthline.com/nutrition/shiitake-mushrooms

Julson, E. (2018, May 19). *9 health benefits of lion's mane mushroom (plus side effects)*. Healthline. https://www.healthline.com/nutrition/lions-mane-mushroom

Kee. (2019). *Wood ear mushrooms salad recipe.* Yummly. https://www.yummly.com/recipe/Wood-Ear-Mushrooms-Salad-9008138#directions

Kiprop, J. (2017, December 21). *Medicinal mushrooms: History and usages.* World Atlas. https://www.worldatlas.com/articles/medicinal-mushrooms-history-and-usages.html

Kodama, N., Komuta, K., & Nanba, H. (2002). Maitake MD-Fraction original research permission. *Alternative Medicine Review X, 7.* https://www.lawankanker.org/wp-content/uploads/2016/05/Can-MD-fraction-aid-cancer-patients.pdf

Kubala, J. (2018, November 6). *5 immune-boosting benefits of turkey tail mushroom.* Healthline. https://www.healthline.com/nutrition/turkey-tail-mushroom

Kubala, J. (2021, May 26). *7 impressive benefits of oyster mushrooms.* Healthline. https://www.healthline.com/nutrition/oyster-mushroom-benefits

La Forge, T. (2018, April 5). *6 mushrooms that act as turbo-shots for your immune system.* Healthline. https://

www.healthline.com/health/food-nutrition/best-medicinal-mushrooms-to-try#for-brain-health

Lin, B., & Li, S. (2011). *Cordyceps as an herbal drug* (I. F. F. Benzie & S. Wachtel-Galor, Eds.). PubMed; CRC Press/Taylor & Francis. https://www.ncbi.nlm.nih.gov/books/NBK92758/

Mayell, M. (2001). Maitake: A premier mushroom maitake extracts and their therapeutic potential. *Alternative Medicine Review X*, 6. http://anaturalhealingcenter.com/documents/Thorne/articles/MaitakeExtract.pdf

Milaonsupplements. (2021, September 12). *How to cook cordyceps: 3 delicious recipes with cordyceps*. Milaonsupplements. https://milaonsupplements.com/supplements/how-to-cook-cordyceps/

Overhiser, S. (2020, December 25). *Lion's mane mushrooms*. A Couple Cooks. Dykes, Timothy (2020). *A log covered in turkey tail mushrooms* [Online Photo]. Unsplash. https://unsplash.com/photos/XPxNvDDYgB4

Sargent, B. (2014, May 25). *Pork dumplings, Asian broth, wood-ear mushrooms*. SBS. https://www.sbs.com.au/food/recipes/pork-dumplings-asian-broth-wood-ear-mushrooms?utm_campaign=yummly&utm_medium=yummly&utm_source=yummly

Sayner, A. (2015, February 2). *5 easy and delicious oyster mushroom recipes*. GroCycle. https://grocycle.com/oyster-mushroom-recipes/

Sayner, A. (2020, February 27). *Hen of the woods (maitake): The ultimate guide*. GroCycle. https://grocycle.com/maitake-mushrooms-guide/

Sayner, A. (2021a, January 15). *A complete guide to reishi mushrooms*. GroCycle. https://grocycle.com/reishi-mushrooms/

Sayner, A. (2021b, April 20). *A complete guide to Chaga mushrooms*. GroCycle. https://grocycle.com/chaga-mushrooms/

Sayner, A. (2021c, April 20). *A complete guide to turkey tail mushrooms*. GroCycle. https://grocycle.com/turkey-tail-mushrooms/

Sayner, A. (2021d, April 30). *Growing lion's mane mushrooms: The ultimate guide*. GroCycle. https://grocycle.com/growing-lions-mane/

Shields, T. (n.d.). *The benefits of cordyceps mushrooms for athletes*. FreshCap Mushrooms. https://learn.freshcap.com/tips/cordyceps-for-athletes/

Shields, T. (n.d.). *Health benefits of maitake: What you need to know about this medicinal mushroom*. FreshCap Mushrooms. https://learn.freshcap.com/tips/health-benefits-of-maitake/

Simple Fit Vegan. (2019, November 12). *The best way to cook shiitake mushrooms.* Simple Fit Vegan. https://simplefitvegan.com/the-best-way-to-cook-shiitake-mushrooms/

Stamets, P., & Zwickey, H. (2014). Medicinal mushrooms: Ancient remedies meet modern science. *Integrative Medicine (Encinitas, Calif.)*, *13*(1), 46–47. https://www.ncbi.nlm.nih.gov/pmc/articles/PMC4684114/

Star Mushroom Farms. (2020, July 31). *How to grow turkey tail mushrooms:[easy way]*. Star Mushroom Farms. https://starmushroomfarms.com/how-to-grow-turkey-tail-mushrooms/#Growing_Turkey_Tail_Mushrooms

Staughton, J. (2016, January 13). *How are mushrooms more similar to humans than plants?* Science ABC. https://www.scienceabc.com/nature/how-are-mushrooms-more-similar-to-humans-than-plants.html

The Green Pages. (n.d.). *The role of mushrooms in nature.* The Green Pages. https://espacepourlavie.ca/en/role-mushrooms-nature

The Times of India. (2018, May 25). *3 ways to tell if a mushroom is poisonous.* The Times of India. https://

REFERENCES | 201

timesofindia.indiatimes.com/life-style/health-fitness/photo-stories/3-ways-to-tell-if-a-mushroom-is-poisonous/photostory/64319824.cms?picid=64319896

Tinsley, G. (2018, March 31). *6 benefits of reishi mushroom (plus side effects and dosage)*. Healthline. https://www.healthline.com/nutrition/reishi-mushroom-benefits#TOC_TITLE_HDR_3

Tiny Plantation. (2017a, May 25). *How to grow shiitake mushrooms in just $5*. Tiny Plantation. https://www.tinyplantation.com/vegetables/mushrooms/how-to-grow-shiitake-mushrooms

Tiny Plantation. (2017b, July 5). *Growing reishi mushrooms - easiest ways to grow in 5 easy steps*. Tiny Plantation. https://www.tinyplantation.com/vegetables/mushrooms/growing-reishi-mushrooms#tab-con-11

Van De Walle, G. (2018, May 9). *6 benefits of cordyceps, all backed by science*. Healthline. https://www.healthline.com/nutrition/cordyceps-benefits

Ware, M. (2019). *Mushrooms: Nutritional value and health benefits*. Medical News Today. https://www.medicalnewstoday.com/articles/278858

Wartenberg, L. (2019, November 11). *Black fungus: Nutrition, benefits, and precautions*. Healthline. https://www.healthline.com/nutrition/black-fungus

Wells, K. (2019, January 7). *Cordyceps mushrooms benefits for anti-aging, endurance & balance.* Wellness Mama. https://wellnessmama.com/395371/cordyceps-benefits/

PHOTO REFERENCES

Dykes, Timothy (2020). *A log covered in turkey tail mushrooms* [Online Photo]. Unsplash. https://unsplash.com/photos/XPxNvDDYgB4

Exebiche (n.d.). *Top view healing chaga mushroom on old birch trunk close up. Red parasite mushroom growth on tree. Bokeh background.* [Online Photo]. Shutterstock. https://www.shutterstock.com/image-photo/top-view- healing-chaga-mushroom-on-1833778705

Frey, Sandra (2017). *Mushroom* [Online Photo]. Unsplash. https://unsplash.com/photos/e9-oSbS-gCE

Horton-Kitchlew, Rachel (2021). *Golden gourmet oyster Mushrooms grown in an urban environment by Designer Rachel Horton-Kitchlew* [Online Photo]. Unsplash. https://unsplash.com/photos/FSLmk8OBhtg

Kornakov, Artur (2021). *Free Fungi Image* [Online Photo]. Unsplash. https://unsplash.com/photos/gqTd5MSZaHc

Machacek, Jaroslav (n.d.). *Edible mushrooms known as Wood ear, Jews ear or Jelly ear (Auricularia auricula-judae) in autumnal forest with blurred background* [Online Photo]. Shutterstock. https://www.shutterstock.com/image-photo/edible-mushrooms-known-wood-ear-jews-524205232

Mamsizz (n.d.). *Dried cordyceps militaris mushroom on wooden spoon* [Online Photo]. Shutterstock. https://www.shutterstock.com/image-photo/dried-cordyceps-militaris-mushroom-on-wooden-500063809

McKay, Jaccob (2020). *Toadstool* [Online Photo]. Unsplash. https://unsplash.com/photos/W-a4ICvpZx4

Photoongraphy (n.d.). *Natural Reishi or lingzhi mushroom growing on old bark* [Online Photo]. Shutterstock. https://www.shutterstock.com/image-photo/natural-reishi-lingzhi-mushroom-growing-on-2097500326

Puttography (n.d.). *Maitake mushroom growing in nature* [Online Photo]. Shutterstock. https://www.shutterstock.com/image-photo/maitake-mushroom-growing-nature-708833389

Zukerman, Yuval (2021). *Organic shiitake mushrooms at the Acton, MA Farmers Market* [Online Photo]. Unsplash. https://unsplash.com/photos/gYGnlltOlx0

Printed in Great Britain
by Amazon